Home Informatics

This One is for the Boffins

Home Informatics

Information Technology and the
Transformation of Everyday Life

Ian Miles

Pinter Publishers, London and New York

First published in Great Britain in 1988 by
Pinter Publishers Limited
25 Floral Street, London WC2E 9DS

British Library Cataloguing in Publication Data

A CIP catalogue record for this book is available from the
British Library

Library of Congress Cataloging-in-Publication Data

Miles, Ian.
   Home informatics.

   'Revision of a report prepared for the Six Countries
Programme on Aspects of Government Policies towards
Technical Innovation in Industry'—Pref.
   Bibliography: p.
   Includes index.
   1. Household electronics.   I. Title.
TK7870.M498   1988   621.381   88-4072
ISBN 0-86187-975-9

Typeset by Florencetype Ltd, Kewstoke, Avon
Printed by Biddles of Guildford Ltd

Contents

List of abbreviations

AT&T	American Telephone and Telegraph
BBC	British Broadcasting Corporation
CAI	Computer-Aided Instruction
CATV	Cable Television
CB	Citizens' Band (radio)
CBS	Columbia Broadcasting System
CD	Compact Disc
CD-I	Interactive Compact Disc
CD-ROM	Read-Only Memory storage system on Compact Disc
CD-V	Compact Disc Video
DAT	Digital Audio Tape Recorder
DBS	Direct Broadcast Satellite
DIY	Do it Yourself
DVI	Interactive Digital Video
EFT	Electronic Funds Transfer
EFTPOS	Electronic Funds Transfer at Point of Sale
EPOS	Electronic Point of Sale Device
GLC	Greater London Council
HDTV	High Definition Television
HI	Home Informatics
HMI	Human-Machine Interface
IBM	International Business Machines Ltd
IHS	Interactive Home Systems
ISDN	Integrated Services Digital Network
IT	Information Technology
LAN	Local Area Network
LED	Light Emitting Diode
LP	Long Playing Record
MAC	Multiplexed Analogue Components
NTT	Nippon Telegraph and Telephone
PSTN	Public Switched Telephone Network
PTT	Telephone & Telecommunications Authority
R&D	Research and Development
RAM	Random Access Memory
RDS	Radio Data Services
ROM	Read-Only Memory
SAN	Small Area Network
TV	Television, television receiver
VCR	Video Cassette Recorder
VDU	Visual Display Unit
VTR	Video Tape Recorder (includes VCRs)
WAN	Wide Area Network
WIMP	human-computer interface based on Windows, Icons, Mouse, and Pull-down/Pop-up menus
WORM	Write Once—Read Many Times

Preface: 'In Three Years, TV as We Know It Will Cease to Exist'

The slogan reprinted above appeared in British colour magazines in the autumn of 1987. Alongside the bold lettering were striking pictures: a satellite and a satellite dish, and a television set with an elongated screen that appeared to be at least a metre long! According to the accompanying blurb, picture quality would be improved by 100 per cent (1250-line screens), and the screen would be four feet wide, three feet high (*not* the dimensions of the illustration!) and thin enough to hang on the wall; 3-D pictures and hi-fidelity stereo sound were also about to arrive.

The advertisement was not actually designed to sell people this new equipment, nor even to whet appetites for it. It was oriented towards producing fear and uncertainty, to make people cautious about buying new goods at the present moment. For the advertisement was sponsored by a TV and radio rentals company, and was attempting to encourage readers to rent rather than buy equipment. The message was: big changes are coming, and you'll be better able to keep up with them by renting systems from us ('rest assured that the moment the latest equipment arrives, we . . . will be there to rent it for you'). So perhaps there is an element of hyperbole in the forecasts. (Is it really plausible that TV as we know it will cease to exist by 1990? Does this correspond to similar cases of product substitution with which we are familiar—after all we still use AM radio. Indeed we still use radio itself alongside TV!)

But evidence that something is certainly going on can readily be found in the other advertisements in these magazines. For example, within a few weeks of the 'In Three Years . . .' advertisement, another full page was announcing that 'The Future Has Arrived'—in other words, why play safe and wait? The new TV being promoted here offers digitised hi-fi stereo sound (70 watts output) and a digitised colour picture with the ability to 'freeze' frames of TV images and to 'zoom in' on parts of pictures or to display 'picture on picture'. It features 'computerised teletext, remote control with personalised memory, dual headphone listening . . . cable, satellite and stereo reception capacilities'. It is, according to the advertisers, 'ready for the future'.

So it does seem that something is happening in the field of consumer electronics. New TVs, and associated devices like satellite dishes, are likewise being promoted. And TV is far from being the only type of consumer equipment where innovations are being promoted. Current advertising media are saturated with microelectronics-based innovations—from 'personal robots' to home security systems, from baby alarms to blood pressure monitors. New consumer products are proliferating.

This book is a survey of this area. It sets out to examine the underlying dynamics of product development, and to specify how technological innovations are likely to develop in coming decades; it attempts to identify the economic and social significance of the wave of new consumer products, and to depict the way in which consumer markets may be shaped. It argues, most fundamentally, that these developments are unduly neglected by most serious analysts, and that it is important to orient more research effort and policy formulation to them.

Like most of my writing, this study has been inspired by several influences. This book is a revision of a report prepared for the *Six Countries Programme on Aspects of Government Policies towards Technical Innovation in Industry*, whose Programme Secretariat is based in the TNO (Organisatie voor Toegepast Natuurwetenschappellijk Onderzoek) at Delft, The Netherlands. The report followed on a workshop organised for the Programme in London (November 1986). (Several of the papers presented at the workshop are to appear in the journal *The Information Society*.) I am particularly grateful to the Programme members for proposing that I help structure the workshop and assess its results, and I would like to thank James Shepherd of the Department of Trade and Industry for his great help and advice in these tasks, and his staff for their organisational support. My then secretary, Valerie Cooke, maintained communications with participants and also helped the smooth running of the workshop.

At the time of writing, I am funded by the PICT (Programme on Information and Communication Technologies) of the Economic and Social Research Council, on a project entitled 'Mapping and Measuring the Information Economy'. The influence of discussions with other project members, as well as with my colleagues at the Science Policy Research Unit, will be apparent to readers familiar with their work. The book is thus an early contribution to the PICT Network, although—in the best 'Home Informatics' tradition—it has actually been written at home in my spare time (on an Atari ST 1040 in First Word Plus, for those interested).

Much of my own research that has entered this study was carried out earlier, however, while I was supported by the Joseph Rowntree Memorial Trust, on a project entitled 'The Future of Work', carried out together with Professor J.I. Gershuny of the University of Bath. This book is thus also intended as a contribution to this project. I would also like to express my considerable gratitude to both the ESRC and the JRMT for their support. (Further publications are being prepared for the ESRC and JRMT projects; a volume on 'Mapping and Measuring the Information Economy' is under way, a book with Gershuny provisionally entitled 'Work in Information Society', and *Information Horizons* (Edward Elgar, forthcoming, 1988) prepared together with H. Rush, K. Turner and J. Bessant).

Further stimulus was provided by projects carried out for the IT EDC of the National Economic Development Office, and for the IRIS project (within the FAST Programme) of the European Community. This essay also draws on interviews conducted together with Graham Thomas, as part of a project funded by the Leverhulme Trust on 'The Emergence of New Interactive Services'.

I owe a great debt to those colleagues mentioned above as sources of ideas, inspiration, and critical feedback. Valuable criticisms have also been provided by Leslie Haddon—at the time of preparing a postgraduate thesis at Imperial College, London, and an anonymous official of the Dutch Ministerie van Economische Zaken (Mr Otto Gorter's Division of Communications and Information Affairs).

1 Introduction

1.1 Why Home Informatics?

The term 'Home Informatics' refers to the applications of Information Technology (IT) products that are emerging for use by members of private households. It covers not only items of *hardware*, like home computers and new consumer electronic goods, but also both the *software* that programmes this equipment, the *services*—such as online information systems (e.g. viewdata)—that may be used with the hardware and software, and the *networks* or systems that are formed by linking together groups of users. It typically applies to IT products used in the home environment, although some other products (for example in-car systems) are sometimes included in the scope of the term.

There has been surprisingly little discussion of consumer electronics developments that are associated with IT. It is almost as if the attitude that such developments are too far removed from the cutting edge of IT to be worth attention prevails; that those who pay attention to them are simply being frivolous. At least, this appears to be the attitude of Western social scientists and journalists; Japanese counterparts appear to take the area rather more seriously.

But it is not just in debates about the 'impacts' of IT that this area is ignored. Most large-scale policy initiatives and intergovernmental programmes in research also ignore the area. They have been centred on 'upstream' applications of, for example, robotics, flexible manufacturing systems, office automation, and the like. Efforts to regulate IT developments—for example by establishing standards—have been dominated by developments in telecommunications (especially ISDN and computer-communications) and factory automation, or by ergonomic considerations aimed at improving workplace conditions. Where new consumer electronics has been an issue of concern, it has been mainly a matter of worries about the loss of employment in electronic assembly operations as product and process innovation has proceeded, with the shift of much production to Asian sites, and of fears about the sparking-off of trade wars by protectionist moves against imports of (notably) videotape recorders and digital audio recorders.

But new consumer electronic products—a fundamental part of what we shall refer to as *Home Informatics* (HI)[1] are worthy of considerable attention, for a number of reasons (these are listed in Table 1.1). These points will be discussed at greater length below. Together, they constitute more than adequate reason for taking a cool look at HI: one that neither assumes that 'in

Table 1.1 Why Home Informatics is an important topic

— A wave of new consumer demand is seen by many as a necessary motor for Western industrialised societies to resume economic growth at rates such as they sustained in the decades immediately following the Second World War.

— Many commentators argue that only consumer markets can provide the outlets for the massive volumes of microelectronic 'chips', the massive power of advanced telecommunications, and other IT capabilities that are expected to come onstream in the medium-term future.

— Already new and improved products from consumer electronics and related industries suggest that a revolution in the 'capital-intensity' of the home as significant in the 'white goods'/'brown goods'/automobile revolution of the post-war decades is in the offing.

— Important firms and government agencies are embarking upon strategies that are designed to shape the contours of HI in directions favourable to themselves.

— Not one, but several, interrelated sectors have interests in the health of new consumer goods and services: these include consumer electronics, broadcasting, household appliances, building and construction services, utilities, the supply industries to all of the above, information organisations such as libraries, etc.

— Trade conflicts have already manifested around HI products such as videotape recorders and digital audio recorders, and there are cultural conflicts around media content; these could well be of considerable scale if the HI market proves to be as dynamic as the above statements suggest.

three years TV as we know it [and much else besides] will cease to exist', nor dismisses this as a non-issue.

1.2 Scepticism and snobbery

However, many—perhaps most—commentators would advocate considerable scepticism about whether consumers will really welcome new domestic applications of IT. The volatility of the market for video games and home computers in recent years is taken as evidence that these are 'fashion markets' or short-run 'crazes'.

For example, in Britain annual home computer sales are currently (1988) less than half of the figure attained in the early 1980s: the market is thus proclaimed to be 'dead', 'merely a fad'. Likewise, the failure of viewdata services—Britain's Prestel, Germany's Bildschirmtext, Canada's Telidon—to achieve anything like the large-scale markets originally forecast for them is seen as showing that there are not really extensive consumer demands for new IT services, that technologists' dreams are far ahead of—or divergent from—consumer realities. (France is admittedly exceptional, but the success of Teletel/Minitel is dismissed as a case of political manipulation: after all, they 'cheated' by giving away terminals and making the service easy to use!) Even cable TV services have displayed only slow progress towards the 'information era' anticipated by futurologists.

Of course, few sceptics would argue that innovation in household equipment has come to a dead stop! Rather, the argument would go that change is more likely to be slow and evolutionary, rather than rapid and discontinuous; that new household goods and services will appear only slowly, that they will typically be elaborations of what we are already familiar with, and that there is simply a lot of premature boosterism going on for products that are not yet really ready to become mass market items.

This argument for scepticism points out that the diffusion of radically new consumer products takes a long time. The white/brown goods/automobile boom of the post-war years was predictable (with hindsight!) in that consumers would already have had a clear view of what equipment they would like, having been exposed to these as elite goods for decades. But nothing equivalent exists yet in respect of HI. There are no very evident products that have proved a success with affluent consumers, and that the rest of us are simply dying to possess once the price falls enough. According to this viewpoint, it will take decades for new information markets to be established, for consumers to have gone through the necessary learning process, and for suppliers to be able to service the new patterns of demand at prices that people will be prepared to pay.

Now, certainly such arguments do need to be taken into account in formulating industrial strategies, government policies and forecasts of the evolution of consumer technology, final demand, and their social implications. They do provide salutary caution against some of the more far-reaching claims of futurologists. But this study will propose that the case for scepticism is overstated, that HI is liable to be of increasing importance. There have indeed been many disappointments in marketing IT-based consumer products. But how should these be interpreted—as evidence that new markets cannot be expected here in the near future, or as providing lessons about the dynamics of consumer acceptance of innovation? It can be suggested, for instance, that some 'marketing failures' have been misinterpreted: for example, the home computer market has not vanished, although there has been a classic industry shake-out. And marketing failures may represent poor marketing rather than intrinsically poor products: for example, most later entrants to the viewdata industry do not seem to have learned from the examples provided by the services that were first on the scene, and have failed to correctly gauge consumer interests.

Furthermore, many HI developments, as we shall see, do not actually depend upon the rapid creation of markets for completely new goods and services. While there are some radically new products, in many instances what is involved is a matter of improving products with which people are already experienced. Consumers are actually quite familiar with product development around white and brown goods. And apart from improvements in, say, TV and audio cassette systems, in cookers and vacuum cleaners, and in cars and telephones, some radically new products in these spheres have been marked successes. That is, they have shown rapid diffusion and the establishment of stable markets in very few years—as is the case, for example, for videotape recorders, Compact Disc players, microwave ovens. These do not appear to be transitory fashion markets.

Another point that may be made in this context is that the new goods and services that are now likely to emerge, often on the back of these modifications of familiar goods and services, do not really involve people undertaking completely new activities. Some improve the convenience with which existing equipment can be used, or the facilities which it provides: video recorders and telephone answering machines are established examples. Others substitute in many respects for familiar household activities: thus video games (and the emerging online computer games) substitute for board games and cards. Other new products, which we shall discuss in detail in due course, may substitute for functions currently provided by manuals, books, audio records, and even for consulting experts and professionals.

The upshot of this is that consumer markets may be less static than the sceptics assume. Indeed, it will be noted in the next chapter that a slow rate of uptake of new consumer products is more likely to look like a break in existing trends than the obvious extension of past experience! It is only too easy to forget just how substantial change in the household economy, and in our leisure activities, has been over the last few decades.

Thus we can conclude that to dismiss HI as mere 'fashion' is inadequate, and that it is not accurate to claim that no new HI products are visible; on the contrary, the volume of change is almost overwhelming. And while some high-tech enthusiasts may adopt a snobbish rather than a sceptical approach, essentially dismissing HI as unworthy of serious consideration, as not really being at the cutting edge of IT innovation, there is no reason to think that the challenges of building good visual displays, speech recognition systems, user-friendly software, and other 'Human-Machine Interface' features are any less for HI than for most commercial and even military applications. Possibly the real obstacle to such erstwhile IT enthusiasts taking HI seriously is really that the latter are unsettled by the rather more competitive market for consumer equipment than for, say, missile guidance systems!

If our rejection of scepticism and snobbery is correct, then attention to the topic of HI is long overdue. Returning to the points made in Table 1.1, the economic issues are important ones. Five sectors are significantly affected by the course of developments:

— consumer electronics itself;
— the sectors supplying components to consumer electronics and related branches of the economy;
— the household appliances sector (and quite possibly related sectors such as building and power supply);
— telecommunications industries, both those based on telephony and those based on broadcasting;
— and the sectors providing 'information services', such as TV and video programme producers, performing artists, librarians, etc.

The failure of major economic powers to maintain a substantial capability in one or more of these sectors may have profound effects on the other sectors, and may well lead to protectionist pressures and a cycle of decline. On the other hand, it can be argued that the development of HI may help revitalise these sectors and lead to a new wave of economic growth based upon expansion of final demand.

However, economic issues are not the only ones at stake, although the social and cultural issues defy easy summary. Various critical voices challenge the ethics of 'creating' new final demand in the industrialised world where there are so many unmet needs in the Third World. Just as IT in general is seen as undermining some trade opportunities for the Third World, it might further be suggested that HI is as much as anything a means for industrialised countries to fight off competition in consumer goods from newly industrialising regions. Other critics are anxious about the content of new media (hard and soft porn? violence? escapism?) and the implications for communities of hi-tech households (privatism? isolation? retreat into fantasy?). There are even portraits of 'electronic feudalism', of a polarisation between IT-based security-guarded affluence and 'bread and circuses' wall-to-wall entertainment to console the (larger or smaller) remainder.

This book cannot hope to establish which of the many competing views of the future is more likely to prove correct. Its aim is more that of providing an interpretation of current and future developments in HI that will shed a little light on the social and technological issues, and thus inform the decision-making that will help shape the future. Even so, we cannot treat all aspects of consumer IT in equal depth: for example, it is likely that in our homes we will have 'smart' cash cards in the next few years: these will be important for shopping behaviour and the retail sector, but are tangential to our main interests and will only be mentioned in passing in this study. (Even so, such cards may even be used in the home to operate pay-TV or similar services!) Likewise, we shall not attempt to cover innovations in our automobiles at any length: the main focus will be on in-home systems.

The five main chapters in this book set out a view of the dynamics of technological development, consumer behaviour, and industrial strategies, and seek to throw light upon future forms and implications of HI. Thus Chapter 2 outlines the scope of HI, and describes general tendencies and technological developments in HI equipment and systems. Chapter 3 considers the demand side of the equation, issues arising in the consumer use of new IT. Chapter 4 discusses the strategies being developed by suppliers of hardware and services, and the innovation and industrial policy issues that arise. Chapter 5 draws on these analyses to investigate future developments in HI, and Chapter 6 summarises the key issues that arise in the course of this discussion, identifying points at which social action may be desirable.

Note

1.   Various alternative terms are in circulation, such as 'new consumer electronics', 'Home Interactive Telematics', 'Home Interactive Systems', 'domotique' etc. Home Informatics has the advantages of being succinct, of making no prejudgements about the role of interactivity or telecommunications, and, not least, of having been the title of the workshop for which the author served as consultant to the Six Countries Programme.

2 From Information Technology to Home Informatics

2.1 Some general tendencies in Home Informatics

In the formal economy, work in both manufacturing and service industries is increasingly subject to a process known by the ugly (but apt) term, 'informatisation'. Activities which were previously directly mediated by human knowledge, perception, recall and reaction have proved to be ideal for the application of IT. In other words, IT is being applied to the information-related aspects of all sorts of work, and since work is carried out by human beings using their consciousness, their perceptions, knowledge and skills, all work has such information-related aspects.

It is worth noting that there are various distinct types of information processing. These may be carried out by the unaided human being, or with the aid of tools and technology. One way of classifying them is to distinguish between:

— production of information (sensing, creating);
— storage and retrieval of information (access);
— transmission and reception of information (communication);
— transforming information (manipulation);
— relating and displaying information (presentation);
— acting on information (actuation).

Technologies have been used to assist human beings in some of these categories of activity at least since systems of visual and nonverbal symbols (writing, flags, drums) were first developed in prehistory.

But more recent technological achievements offer tremendous scope for the transformation of traditional ways of carrying out these activities. IT, largely based on digital information processing via microelectronics and optronics, involves dramatic increases in the applicability of technology to *all* of these aspects of information processing. In its short history, IT has achieved tremendous improvements in physical performance. No doubt readers will be familiar with the exponential-type trend lines that are revealed when features like chip density, RAM capacity, or channel capacity are plotted over time.[1]

This increasing power of IT means that the new technologies are increasingly offering a number of key features, depicted in Table 2.1. These features give IT the vast scope for application noted above; it can be applied to many areas of economic activity that have previously been relatively unaffected by technological change on the grounds of cost, cumbersomeness, or lack of

Table 2.1   Key features of Information Technology

● *Decreasing cost of information processing.*
The costs of data storage, transmission, manipulation, etc. have been falling
rapidly for decades, which means that bulk data processing or very complex
operations that would heretofore have been unthinkable can now be carried out.

● *Decreasing size of equipment.*
This means that new technology can be incorporated unobtrusively into existing
devices, or installed in locations where large artefacts would have rendered the
application unviable.

● *Speedier information processing.*
This is largely a result of overcoming the batch-processing system, but also
reflects more rapid data transmission and more integrated systems; it means that
time-sensitive operations can be carried out, and that irritating delays are
reduced.

● *Increased reliability of equipment.*
There are fewer mechanical components and non-integrated components to go
wrong, and applications are thus less prone to breakdown (although, when they
do so, they are usually not user-repairable).

● *Increased quality and user-friendliness of systems.*
This results from 'surplus' processing power being incorporated in displays,
menus, error-checking routines, etc., and greater emphasis on 'human factors' in
the design of systems for use by non-expert users.

● *Distributed rather than centralised information processing facilities become available.*
This means that the processing power of the terminal may outstrip that
previously possessed by the host, and has significant consequences for the
location of operations.

● *Digitalisation of data and information of all sorts.*
This means that information generated in one medium can be more readily
transferred to different media (thus the same material may be embodied as a
printed journal, or as 'hypertext' on CD-ROM, or as source material on online
databases).

● *Increased importance of 'software' of all kinds (including texts and broadcasts, etc.).*
There has been a relatively large increase in the costs of professional production
of software (especially as contrasted with decreasing hardware costs) and a
massive decrease in reproduction costs.

skills. IT can also be applied in new ways: the wider availability of the equipment makes possible innovative applications of many kinds. The technologies radically alter the scope for technological support to information processing in many activities, making it possible to engage in, for example, more detailed control of process operation and product design. The application of technology does not merely substitute for jobs carried out by human beings (or earlier generations of technology): it makes possible activities that were previously out of the question.

Thus IT is diffusing widely across the sectors of the formal economy; it is a 'heartland technology', which changes the 'common sense' of production and work organisation.[2] It is being applied to many work processes—from supermarket check-outs to aircraft assembly, from brain surgery to driving taxis—and not just to the so-called 'information occupations' whose main task is information processing or whose main product is information. But this is work in the formal economy: what about IT and informal, household, work, and in leisure activities?

In the formal economy, the cheapening of information processing means that there can be major innovations in the production process. IT can be used to consult stored knowledge, to record new data, to operate equipment on the basis of signals received and programmes installed, to communicate across long distances, and to perform statistical and other analyses. And it is often possible to do this in ways that are not notably time- and money-consuming, nor skill-intensive and laborious. While the motives of, and constraints upon, consumers are far from identical with those applying to organisations in the formal economy, similar sorts of innovation may be anticipated in the informal domestic economy.

Despite scepticism about the prospects for HI, it is clear that IT can be applied to the informal work carried out within private households, often in much the same way as it can be applied to formal work. The sceptics assume that because consumers appear to acquire relatively low volumes of information from the formal economy, and use little technology to process information in the course of their household activities, there is little scope for the application of IT here. But all current household activities do depend on information processing (inspecting circumstances, forming judgements and acting on perceptions), and the use of accumulated knowledge (information storage and retrieval, perhaps simply from memory but sometimes consulting books, timetables maps, etc.), and many involve communications.

Let us outline just two examples. Housework activities like cooking may involve frequent inspection of the cooking process, control of the oven and other tools being used, and a combination of skills and, perhaps, advice and instructions drawn from recipe books. (There may also be communication with family members, either directly or by telephone, concerning when people are likely to arrive for the meal.) Leisure activities also involve information processing. Home entertainment frequently involves not just the use of mass media, but also the consultation of newspaper listings of

programme schedules, the retrieval of information from LP records or
videotapes, the storage of information on audio or videotapes, etc.

Already in the home environment there are many technologies (not all IT!)
that perform informational functions. Figure 2.1 presents a picture of the
broadening spectrum of consumer electronics, based entirely on products
that are already widely diffused in one or more Western countries. It suggests

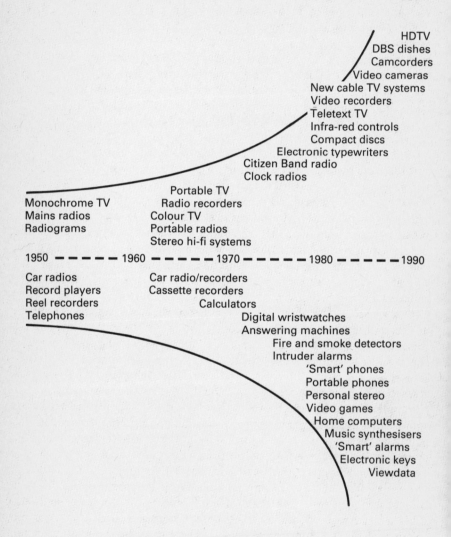

Figure 2.1   The widening spectrum of consumer electronics products

Note: This diagram was inspired by and is partly based on MacKintosh (1984). It should be
noted that the dates are very approximate and vary from country to country.

Application area	Established technology	Digital system	Further developments
Messaging	Mail, telephony	Electronic mail, telephony, viewdata, etc. on ISDN digital system	Broadband ISDN
Audio	LP records	CD systems	Interactive and video CD (CD–I, –V)
	Audio cassette	Digital audio tape	Advanced digital audio and video systems, disc and tape
Video	Video cassette	Digital video tape	
	(Video disc)	(CD–V)	
Broadcast audio and video	TV, radio	Teletext TV. Digital audio and video data processing	Radiotext, digital broadcasts
Information production	Clocks, metres and displays	Digital clocks, metres, displays	
			Automated interactive equipment
Actuation	Mechanical and electro-mechanical controls	Keyboard-type controls	

Figure 2.2   The digitalisation of household technologies

Source: Modified from Figure 5.5 of Miles, Rush, Turner and Bessant (1988).

that consumer product innovation has been proceeding for many decades, and sceptics about HI might do well to reflect on whether they are really expecting this trend to come to a halt!

Within the contemporary household in Western societies, then, are devices that:

Table 2.2   Main directions of IT application to consumer products

— *An improvement in the effectiveness, quality or power* of many consumer technologies. For example, better sound or video reproduction, higher levels of data storage, more versatile telephones. In many respects these involve improvements in the 'Human-Machine Interface' which render devices more user-friendly and suitable for mass markets (discussed in Section 2.2).

— *The addition of new functions* to equipment. For example, being able to meter new things, being able to obtain more useful information from meters, being able to communicate in circumstances where this has been previously impossible (discussed in Section 2.3).

— *The development of new types of equipment.* For example, home computers, videotape recorders, Compact Disc systems are already familiar (discussed in Section 2.4).

— *The integration of many functions*, as the possibility of different items of equipment easily and cheaply intercommunicating allows for useful applications of integration to be implemented. Examples include TVs being able to carry alarm messages from home security devices or from malfunctioning equipment, power-consuming devices being controlled by electricity meters according to tariff rates (discussed in Section 2.5). ·

— *transmit* information into and out of the home (mail, newspapers, radio and TV, telephones have all supplemented word-of-mouth communication and personal transport);
— *monitor and/or control* the operations of domestic equipment (metres, dials and displays, and even fuses which respond to abnormally high power loads);
— *store* information for subsequent reproduction and display (notepads and photographs have been supplemented by audio and videotapes);
— *manipulate* information, amplifying signals and allowing for transformations of audio and video outputs, performing mathematical and other processes (audio 'equalisers' and synthesisers supplement sound systems, calculators displace mental arithmetic, 'smart' tools perform tasks more effectively).

IT-based innovation is already beginning to have an impact on these technologies. Often, what is involved is a transfer of technologies developed for industrial (or military) applications to consumer purposes. And often we are seeing digital IT devices substituting for—and augmenting—previous household information and communication systems. Figure 2.2 outlines the developments here—unfamiliar terms will be explained in due course. Table

2.2 then goes on to set out the most notable features of IT-based innovation in terms of improvements to consumer goods and services.

There are several overlaps among the four types of innovation listed in Table 2.2, of course, but for convenience we shall discuss them in the order in which they have been presented above. The first point will be divided into three items: improved controls and displays, improved data storage and retrieval, and improved communication facilities.

2.2 Improvements in existing functions

2.2.1 Improved controls and displays

The improvement of controls and displays is already widely apparent: on more modern items of equipment, controls are often push-button or even touch switches, while information on the state of apparatus is supplied in the form of numerical data on an LED or liquid crystal display. There has been a shift from traditional mechanical and electromechanical dials and switches, to electronic and microelectronic ones, just as the controls within devices have also moved in this direction. These shifts parallel developments in industrial equipment, and a general feature of innovation in consumer products is that it frequently represents a technology transfer in which systems developed for industrial use are adapted to home applications (as discussed in more detail in the following chapter).

Often, the improvements in displays are accompanied by *improved quality in the information that is yielded*. For example, they may provide not only more readable, but also more precise, data (e.g. seconds as well as hours and minutes). Frequently, additional low-cost informational functions are added (thus digital clocks, for example, are standard in many radios, microwave cookers, video recorders). And, corresponding to increasingly precise data outputs, more precise inputs can also be accommodated. One reason for incorporating clocks in many gadgets is to be able to use these to automatically control cooking times or the recording of TV programmes; and these can be controlled with great precision.

Other features of controls and displays are also quite well established already. IT is often claimed to liberate users from traditional limitations of time and space: because information can be stored and transmitted readily, the user need no longer be at the right place at the right moment to make use of a facility. This is most clear in the development of 'teleservices' (telebanking, teleshopping, etc.), but also already applies to the controls on domestic equipment in a modest way.

Remote control by hand-held infra-red devices is common for TV and hi-fi systems, and is also becoming available for some other devices. (For example, it is possible to operate some microcomputer keyboards at a distance from the VDU and other bulky components, so that, for example, the keyboard may be operated in one's lap from an armchair, rather than on a table or desktop.) Telephone answering machines can be interrogated by their owners from distant locations, by sending the appropriate tone over the phone.

Programmability has long been a gimmicky feature of household appliances like washing, knitting and sewing machines. In the main, this has really consisted of a number of pre-existing options being made available, so that they can be chosen by appropriately setting a dial or pressing buttons. Occasionally there has been external 'software', in the form of a card—this is of course not electronic but mechanical software, rather like a music roll was software to drive a pianola. More recently, electronic and microelectronic systems have enabled devices to operate with more flexibility. More preprogrammed options are available on current washing machines, for example. Record and tape players need not just play the (ROM) software of the LP or tape, but can search for particular tracks and play them in a chosen order; and to the conventional tone and volume controls are added so-called graphic equalisers, that allow for more precise adjustment of the sound output to the features of one's room or to one's personal tastes.

Each of these trends in controls and displays is accelerated considerably by the application of IT. The low cost of microelectronics, and the use of the technology within devices, means that improvements in these 'Human-Machine Interfaces' (HMIs) can form a relatively cheap way of improving products. Thus we can expect to see further innovation in the capability to operate domestic equipment at a distance, to have it controlled by inputs that do not require one's immediate physical presence, in its programmability to suit personal needs and tastes, and in the quality of the information that is provided for users.

For example, the author was recently shown a prototype system based around a wall-mounted electroluminescent touch-sensitive screen. This compact, extremely thin visual display unit (VDU) presented information in a variety of modes, the starting-point being a 'menu'-type invitation to users to select among options by simply pressing the appropriate part of a touch-sensitive screen. The options in this example included controlling devices in various rooms (for example adjusting the temperature to which the radiators are to bring a given room), and accessing information stored in various ways (electronic notepad and telephone directory). The screen could also function as a typewriter-type keyboard, for example for inputting messages into the notepad. The device was neat and unobtrusive. It exemplified the combination of innovations involving (1) Informative visual displays to output information and (2) user-friendly means of inputting information without needing keyboard or programming skills.[3]

Another type of control device involves improving existing infra-red remote control systems—for example so that they are able to operate several devices rather than being dedicated to just one. Such infra-red controls (apparently known in Italy by the picaresque term 'auto-commando;') are also featuring improved types of key and button, so that they can be used more easily and precisely. Several companies are known to be developing such multi-purpose controllers.

But screens and finger-presses are not the only means of controlling and monitoring devices. In applications in the formal economy, *voice synthesis* is being used to provide some types of information, such as the prices of items being passed before a bar-code Electronic Point of Sale (EPOS) device. Similar innovations are apparent in some consumer goods, for example warning systems in cars to inform drivers if seat belts are undone or if oil is running low, and 'speaking clocks' that announce the hour. (The latter is an example of an application that may be particularly suitable for blind people. It should be noted that efforts to overcome or at least offset disabilities could well often form the focus of specific HI innovations which may later be adapted to a wider consumer market.) Spoken output from equipment may be most appropriate where very simple data is provided or where urgent action is required, at least until speech synthesis can be made to sound more natural, and the information can be put into a form more closely resembling natural language.

Speech recognition on the part of equipment, beyond an extremely basic kind, seems further away; it is relatively costly, requiring high data-processing power and much research is under way around the appropriate software. However, microcomputers which can recognise a fairly large vocabulary have already been developed, though they need to be 'trained' to understand each speaker, and at present are mainly used in high-value specialist applications (e.g. to enable engineers checking aircraft to keep a record of points they have noticed, without needing to use their hands) and by top executives. Over the coming decades the techniques for this sort of HMI will no doubt be vastly improved and cheapened. Speech-driven controls, that can accept verbal commands as a basis for operation, together with speech synthesis and systems that can process natural language (a goal of the Japanese Fifth Generation Programme) will ultimately allow for interaction between user and equipment to take place using natural language rather than single commands or restricted phrases; and with devices having the capacity to ask for clarification if there seem to be mistakes, misunderstandings, or ambiguous and insufficiently specified instructions.

A further development might be termed '*telecontrol*'. This involves the ability to interact with remote devices, for example by telephone. Already, for example, some directory enquiry and mail order systems are able to process simple inputs from users, and to provide appropriate answers or set other procedures into operation. Domestic equipment may similarly be turned on or off, or interrogated as to its status, by telephone. An alternative form of within-home communication is termed 'peritelevision', and involves equipping devices so that they can send messages as to their status to the domestic TV. The wall-hanging VDU system described earlier is a display/control device dedicated to these functions.[4]

The issue of user-friendliness, which underlies efforts to develop menu-driven systems and speech recognition, reflects a problem that seems to be increasingly common. Simply put, it is that the 'new freedom' of consumer choice may present an information overload. Having to make too many choices can be insufferable, especially if the end-results will be pretty similar in any case—or if many of the options are quite irrelevant to one's foreseeable requirements. The example of the fast food outlet where more time is spent choosing between the innumerable combinations of bread, filling, garnishes and drinks than is taken to prepare the meal is a case in point. In practice, consumers may not always want high levels of feedback, wide spectra of choice.

It appears that part of the success of modern cameras and music centres is that they relieve users of choices which may be time-consuming and knowledge-demanding. It is far easier to just point a camera in the right direction and press the button, to load a tape or CD into the music centre and press a button than it is to be a photography or hi-fi enthusiast, and most of us have a range of enthusiasms that is more limited than our range of tastes. The two examples are worth pursuing; they point to rather different aspects of the problem, and indicate rather different solutions.

Thus, microprocessor-controlled cameras can actually make many of the operating decisions for the user; they ensure a higher proportion of successful shots than inexperienced photographers are liable to achieve (though use of these functions may rule out some special effects and more creative photography). (A parallel innovation is under way in microwave cookers, into which some manufacturers are now placing sensors that weigh foodstuffs and monitor temperatures so as to achieve optimum results, relieving users of the need to make rule-of-thumb estimates.) Music centres relieve consumers of the need to make decisions about the technical and aesthetic compatibility of different items of hi-fi equipment, and thus provide an integrated 'package' of components. Although there may be inflexibility and costs in this approach (the system may well need to be repaired or replaced as a whole), it is likely to provide reproduction as well as any combination of items amounting to the same price. And, hobbyists apart, it is the final service provided, the quality of output supplied, that is being bought, not the specific technologies that are involved.

The evolution of HI is liable to involve a large number of trade-offs of this kind—trade-offs between 'information overload' and flexibility of operation. With the advent of devices that are more truly programmable, we may expect to see domestic equipment following the path taken by user-friendly microcomputer systems, presenting a variety of preset or default options, being capable of operating in default mode with no lengthy instructions, but having the capability of accepting—and storing for future reference—our own peculiar requirements. Eventually, we may anticipate appliances that can learn from our reactions to past operations, so as to 'guess' our preferences.

2.2.2 Improved data storage and retrieval

A story (which is perhaps apocryphal) describes well a major limitation of the first wave of HI devices. It tells of an elderly lady encountered in one of the first displays of home computers in a high street store. After fingering a keyboard for a few moments, she was heard to mutter 'what good are these computers if they can't tell me what the price of eggs is?'

The story underlines the point that the practical uses of high-powered information processing devices are very much limited by what information they have available to process. A (non-apocryphal) story illustrates the point further. The author was recently present at a library demonstration of a CD-ROM encyclopaedia. The librarian's summation was: 'First-rate information technology, fourth-rate information'.

Presvelou's (1986b) study of home computer users also illustrates this point well: users who input large volumes of data themselves were usually motivated by a professional interest (e.g. those preparing texts via word processing) or a hobby (indexing their stamp collection, for example). Otherwise, users would be largely interested in exploring the computer in order to learn programming skills, or to play games. The tedium of typing in facts and figures makes current home computers a poor choice for many home tasks, and there have been few commercially-available databases that appeal to home users. Perhaps the most common reaction to this situation within the IT industry has been to advocate access to data via tele-communication as the answer: home computers will come into their own, it is suggested, when linked to viewdata systems that can provide near-instantaneous access to any of a large number of huge databases.

Before turning to telecommunication possibilities, however, which we will do in Section 2.2.3, we should consider developments in data storage and retrieval systems. One of the most interesting features of the emerging HI field is the co-evolution of 'privatique' (stand-alone devices) and 'telematique' (networked systems). Often these are seen as competing systems, which to a considerable extent they are, but by the term co-evolution we seek to draw attention to the following features of their interrelationship:

— First, data access via local data storage devices and telecommunications are to some extent in competition, with users faced with a choice between two modes of access to similar types of data. The two modes of access do have different design characteristics, which affect the choice: for example, the costs of equipment and use of the database, the degree to which the data have been kept up to date, etc.

— Second, this competitive process leads to technological innovation around the two systems, taking the form of efforts to capitalise on the design characteristics of the different modes—for example, by establishing market niches where negative features are less important, or by

efforts to overcome these features. This can lead to a proliferation of different media within each system.
— Third, the two systems may develop symbiotic relationships, so that the diffusion of one may actually facilitate that of its apparent competitor. For example, 'telematique' databases may be designed so that their material can be quickly and cheaply downloaded into a 'privatique' storage medium.

We shall discuss data storage and retrieval systems in some details since developments here are moving rather rapidly, following a period in which attention was more often directed to viewdata and similar telecommunications systems.

The terminology used to describe data storage in computer systems can be applied to traditional consumer goods. Conventional audio records (and now Compact Discs) are ROM (read-only memory) devices; the data they contain may be degraded, but it cannot be modified in any useful way. The same is effectively true of printed materials, although readers may jot in the margins or fill in crosswords! Audio and now videotapes are RAM (random access memory), in that data may be recorded and erased repeatedly on the same medium—rather like a blackboard. Less familiar are WORM (write once read many times) media, which allow users to add data but which only permit these to be added to (up to the limits of capacity of the medium), not to be rewritten. A conventional notebook (without an effective eraser) is effectively a WORM system, as is photographic film.

As the examples suggest, many storage media are already in common use in the domestic environment. The most important developments that are under way concern advances in the storage and retrieval of large volumes of data encoded in digital form. Compact Discs (CDs) are the best-known example of such media at present, although digital tape recorders and digital VTRs are now in production. CDs use optical technology, with data recorded in the form of dots—digital information—which are read by laser light. This enables massive quantities of information to be stored on a small disc. First made familiar through audio CD systems for domestic use, CD is proving a powerful means of storing large databases for computer use: thus, many 'electronic publishers' providing online information services for business users are now making their data available on CD. This data storage for microcomputer use is generally referred to as CD-ROM, to distinguish it from the use of CD for audio storage. CD-WORM systems are currently considerably more expensive than CD-ROM, and have a correspondingly limited market. Completely erasable and rewriteable CD systems are also being developed, but are unlikely to be cheaply available for some time yet.

Where the information is not such as to require rapid and frequent undating, optical ROM systems have proved a viable approach, especially as costs of CD-ROM systems have come within the reach of even small

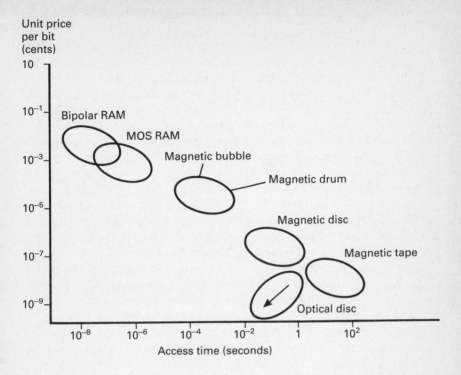

Figure 2.3 Features of various storage media in the late 1980s

Source: Philips (1986), p. 6.

businesses; they are currently comparable with the costs of Winchester hard disc systems, but can store over 600 megabytes of data as compared to the 10–30 megabytes typical of hard discs. Furthermore, this is not just an application relevant to wealthy business environments. For example, it is already posible for libraries to acquire a CD version of a large encyclopaedia (the Graunier encyclopaedia, with several volumes on a single disc), which is also promoted as being suitable for home education purposes. This system is not just a book read from a VDU; it also offers the possibility of vastly improved indexing functions, so a full-text search for the occurrence of particular words or phrases is possible. A CD-ROM system permits a microcomputer to access large volumes of data which are stored in a robust, transportable and secure form (it is predicted that disc life will be in excess of ten years in the typical office); and, while data retrieval from the system is somewhat slower than from conventional 'hard discs', this is being improved. Figure 2.3 compares price and access times for a variety of storage media; it is apparent that optical media are capable of vastly cheaper mass data storage than their main competitors, and that they are becoming equivalently speedy in operation.

An educational application of videodisc (rather than CD) technology has also been attracting considerable attention. This is also of interest in that videodiscs were initially launched as consumer systems, and the fate of the original product is relevant to the analysis of consumer choices around HI that we carry out in Chapter 3. Despite the high-quality reproduction of video images by videodiscs, these were beaten in the marketplace by VTRs, largely because the latter system allowed for recording of TV transmissions for later viewing, whereas the former required hire or purchase of pre-recorded material.

The educational application in question is Britain's 'Domesday Project', consisting of two videodiscs to be used with a Philips interactive videodisc player and a BBC microcomputer. The system (on two discs) presents an hour of video film material, but it also contains tens of thousands of maps, tens of thousands of still photographs, and over one hundred thousand videotext 'pages' of information, together with material from the British census and the parliamentary record. Users can 'zoom' in on local areas from national maps, take 'walks' through a number of visual environments, call up census or survey data for processing, and search for material on a wide range of topics. Further videodiscs under preparation are also oriented to education (and training), although some are being developed as new types of in-store shopping catalogue.

This system is relatively expensive (costing around £4000, although the manufacture of each disc costs a mere £5). However, cost reductions are likely as the technology matures, and the key feature of interactivity is seen as central to the evolution of similar CD systems. Current audio CD is largely the passive replaying of data stored in a linear sequence (although it is possible to select tracks in particular orders, etc., as noted earlier). The concept of interactive CD systems (CD-1) proposes access to the large volumes of data that may be stored on CD for a wide variety of purposes, not just those currently associated with CD-ROM systems, as became available for micro-computers in the mid-1980s.[5] Building on existing CD standards and the mass production of CD players for the consumer market (over 10 million have been shipped—well in excess of industry forecasts), the aim is to establish mass markets for the more advanced CD-I systems.

The CD can be used to store information of various kinds and at various levels of quality. For example, instead of one hour of stereo hi-fidelity audio, some seven hundred hours of phonetic speech could be on tap (and, in fact, even a CD of current capacity would be capable of storing three thousand still pictures of higher quality than current TV pictures alongside an hour of stereo music). Like audio material, visual images (including text) can be stored at various level of definition (and with possibilities for different numbers of colours being used). Simple animation is easily possible, and even true 'motion picture' video images can be handled, though there are currently limitations on this (which will be discussed further in Chapter 4). Thus CD-I will make use of audio and video data like current home entertainment media; but it will also be able to use computer data like CD-ROM systems. Potential applications—discussed at greater length in Chapter ·5—include: new types of interactive book (e.g. speaking dictionaries, electronic encyclopaediae and Do It Yourself manuals for home use), databases, games and entertainment, media for music and graphics composition, and practical tools such as roadmap displays for motorists.

Thus, major developments are under way in data storage and retrieval systems for home use. (We have, of course, only discussed the media themselves: the matter of rendering content, 'software', in a form suitable for them is another matter again. Skills are scarce when it comes to making effective use of media that offer interactivity rather than linear access, that freely mix text, audio, graphics, etc. A new sort of 'editing and publishing' industry is emerging to cope with these novel tasks.) Let us now turn to telecommunications, which is often regarded as the competing means of accessing databases—but, equally if not more importantly, also permits HI to be used for the interrogation of remote devices, and for interpersonal communications and messaging.

2.2.3 Improved communications

Three major developments may be cited here; they will be discussed sequentially in this subsection. They are:

— First, the upgrading of the telecommunications infrastructure, as exemplified by the use of Direct Broadcast Satellites (DBS), the creation of new cable TV networks using technology far superior to the traditional coaxial cables, and the replacement of existing telephone systems by the integrated Services Digital Network (ISDN) framework.
— Second, the emergence of new telecommunications services and improved telecommunicatiaons devices, such as viewdata and electronic mail, cellular radio and portable telephones.
— Third, the development of in-house communications systems—which appear to be moving on rapidly from familiar and limited types of remote control devices and baby alarms to 'Small Area Networks' (SANs). (The term 'Small Area Network' was coined to contrast these systems with the Local Area Networks of business establishments and the Wide Area Networks such as national telephone systems.)

These systems all reflect the novel developments that have given rise to Information Technology: IT is often defined as 'the convergence of computers and telecommunications'. Increasingly information processing and transmission are taking advantage of the superior features of digitalisation.

Thus the ISDN allows for the transmission of all types of data through the same network. Conventional telephone systems allow for a variety of telephone voice services (with fairly low-quality sound reproduction), together with low-speed telex, facsimile, viewdata and other computer data communications. The latter may be routed through Packet Switch Stream Services, which take advantage of digitalisation to reduce costs and increase error-trapping, but in most countries a modem is still necessary to 'translate' digital computer data into a form suitable for conveying on the analogue telephone system. The ISDN systems now under construction are intended to allow for much more rapid data transmission, and will be able to digitalise voice communications. The increased capacity of ISDN systems—which most Western advanced industrial nations are planning to install by the mid-1990s—will permit substantially better telecommunications services, such as photovideotex (near-photographic quality viewdata images), to be delivered. And the digitalisation of operations should improve the quality of services, with less noise and more error-trapping on the line.

ISDN is being promoted for several reasons, not the least being the increased reliance of enterprises on telecommunications, and their desire to communicate large volumes of data across national boundaries with minimum inconvenience. It is also believed by many planners that an improved telecommunications network will be the basis for the emergence of many new telecommunications-based services, and thus for a rapid expansion of demand for use of the networks. However, even ISDN is far from the broadband system that futurologists have typically envisaged as the 'data highway' of the 'information society', and some commentators argue that, for a really dynamic development of new services, more radical steps need to be taken. The channel capacity envisaged for the public networks (64 kilobits per second) is, in particular, too low for the transmission of moving video images as required for videophones or TV transmission. (Some slow-scan video images may be conveyed on ISDN, and even on existing networks: examples include security applications and a primitive videophone that has recently been displayed under the name 'teleport'.[6]) It is also too low for some data-intensive business telecommunications, but firms requiring such facilities at present are typically large organisations able to lease private lines of high capacity.

Optical fibre systems have the capacity to carry information at levels *millions* of times higher than that of the ISDN plans. Table 2.3 indicates the evolution of capabilities of conventional, ISDN and broadband communications in terms of the types of service they can carry—though it should be noted that improved information processing techniques (signal compression, etc.) are widening the capabilities of conventional systems.

Optical fibres are now commonly used by telecommunications companies for their trunk lines and international connections. Some countries—notably Japan and West Germany—are planning to introduce optical communications to residential users over the coming years, and other countries—notably

Table 2.3 Evolutionary stages in the services handled by telecommunications systems

---

1. Conventional Systems

TELEPHONE	Conventional telephones, mobile phones, cellular phones
FACSIMILE	Low-speed facsimile
STILL PICTURES	Viewdata (videotext)
MOTION PICTURES	'Teleport' (very slow updating of video pictures for primitive videophone etc)
TEXT	Telex, teletex, electronic mail, online databases
DATA	Packet switch-stream communications, low-speed data communications via modem

2. ISDN System (64k bits/sec)

TELEPHONE	Digital telephone services including digitised voice (suitable for packet switching and voice storage), additional display data on phones (charges, numbers accessed), messaging, voice synthesis, information services
FACSIMILE	Digital facsimile (enabling more speed and communication between different device types)
STILL PICTURES	Digital viewdata (more rapid, voice as well as display, more detailed display), telewriting (remote display of handwritten information)
MOTION PICTURES	Slow-scan video communications (suitable for surveillance and security purposes, etc), animated viewdata
TEXT	Leased circuits, retrieval of stored information, mixed text and voice transmission
DATA	Leased circuits, circuit-switching, Electronic Funds Transfer system, telemetry, alarms

3. Broadband System

TELEPHONE	Hi-fi sound
FACSIMILE	Ultra-high-speed and precise colour facsimile
STILL PICTURES	High quality viewdata (35mm photo standard)
MOTION PICTURES	Video telephones, video conferencing, standard and high-definition TV
TEXT	Rapid bulk text transmission, quality teletex services
DATA	High-speed computer-communications

Source: Drawing on Evans *et al.* (1983), Miles *et al.* (1988) and Stallings (1984).

France—have been experimenting with 'optically wired' communities. In other cases—for example Britain—the more advanced cable TV systems that have been installed use optical cables. Such systems offer facilities unthinkable on conventional cable TV. For example, the Westminster Cable system in London, as well as offering twenty TV channels and viewdata and teleshopping services, permits users to choose which of a hundred (plans are to increase this to a thousand) films on store in a central video library they wish to have transmitted to their home TV set.

Britain has followed a policy which effectively hopes that such privately-owned and entertainment-based cable TV systems will be the basis for the development of 'data highways'. But many commentators are sceptical of the idea that market forces alone can rapidly establish a widespread broadband system. There are thus pleas for governmental action to speed the pace of telecommunications development. Several Europeans—including some members of the European Community—argue for 'Eurogrid', an inter-governmental effort to set up such a system. (The concept has even been taken up by Britain's opposition Labour Party. A sustained case for 'Eurogrid' is made by Mackintosh (1986).) The justifications for such proposals vary, but the two most common are (1) that this will provide an incentive for the European IT industry to consolidate its inovative efforts and (2) that such a system is a necessary feature of 'information society', the infrastructure required for a wide variety of new IT-based goods and services to be developed and to find adequate markets.

Whatever the pace of change, it is clear that the telecommunications power available to private households will increase in coming decades. Access to telephony and computer-communications via the public telephone network, to broadcast TV via Direct Broadcast Satellites (DBS) and via cable TV (which, as noted, can also provide 'narrowcast' services) is growing.

The capabilities of home reception/transmission equipment are also growing: devices are becoming smaller and more portable, memories are being installed, and the multi-telephone, multi-TV home is becoming as common now as the multi-radio home became shortly after the advent of the cheap transistor radio. This reflects the use of microelectronic components and the digitalisation of at least some of the information processing activities in home equipment. This is taking place in advance of the digitalisation of telephone, radio and TV transmissions (as opposed to the recordings that are transmitted), which is only just beginning.

Many new telecommunications services have been introduced to the mass market in the last decade (see Table 2.4). We shall return to such new services in more depth later. But, in addition to telecommunications which relate the home to remote information sources, in-home communications are becoming more important.

A number of communications media are already in use by domestic devices:

Table 2.4 New telecommunications services

— *Broadcast information services*. Teletext transmission to television sets has widely diffused in a number of Western countries; this enables viewers to call up 'pages' of information (e.g. news services, broadcasting schedules), and can also be used to provide, for example, subtitles for the hard-of-hearing and different language groups. A rather similar system for radio broadcasts, Radio Data Services, is currently in the late stages of development and prototyping: its main uses are likely to be the transmission of emergency messages and codings representing the class of programme currently broadcast.

— *Interactive Telematics*. The best-known system here is videotext (viewdata), which can be used like teletext to gain access to remote databases (but with a wider selection), but can also be used for transactional services (teleshopping, telebooking, etc.), and for message services (electronic mail, chatlines, etc.). Other forms of electronic mail and online services like games have also established niche consumer markets.

— *New telephone services*. While message storing and similar services are mainly oriented to business users, new services for consumers include numerous stored messages (weather forecasts, information on AIDS, etc.) and 'Talkabout' facilities (which enable callers to join in group discussions in a telephone equivalent of Citizens' Band radio).

— infra-red signals as used by the 'auto-commando', remote controls for TVs and the like;
— mains signalling by some baby alarms (these feature sound detectors that plug into an electricity mains socket in the baby's room, and set off signalling devices similarly located in the living room or elsewhere);
— radio, as used by some security devices and by portable telephones;
— and specialised wiring as used in most other alarm and security devices and by 'distributed' entertainment systems (the most recent Bang and Olafsen systems feature infra-red controls and coaxial wiring to carry the high-fidelity audio).

There are thus numerous physical media available for in-home communications. An important direction for the development of HI, as we shall see below, involves using these to allow household devices to intercommunicate. The existing electrical mains is exploited as an existing 'infrastructure' in mains signalling. This only allows for the transmission of limited volumes of data, but, for instance, this is quite sufficient for signals concerning the state of apparatus, and for the transmission of messages instructing devices to turn on or off. A major problem that is confronted by mains signalling is that the mains network is not confined to a single home, that various coding techniques are required to prevent interference with neighbours' apparatus.

Radio and infra-red transmission require no rewiring and permit not only physical mobility on the part of users (within quite different limits!), but also allow for considerably higher levels of data transmission than does mains signalling. Although problems of interference arise again, standards have been developed for cordless phones and related devices that should provide a basis for overcoming these. Cable and wiring systems can convey massive quantities of data (depending upon the type of cable used—optical fibres can carry vastly more data than coaxial or conventional wires), but require installation of new systems within houses.

All of these systems are under active investigation by manaufacturers of consumer electronics and other interested parties. (For example, electricity supply companies are very interested in the prospects for mains signalling.) Technological developments in these media, together with increases in the capability and utility of intercommunication on the part of domestic equipment, mean that IT is liable to increase the importance of in-house communications systems (SANs) at the same time that it is revolutionising telecommunications (WANs).

2.3 New capabilities

Our second point was the addition of *radically new functions* to domestic equipment. An example of this which has already been mentioned is the addition of teletext capabilities to ordinary domestic TV sets. This is now a common, if not yet standard, feature in several Western countries. In this case the new function is (typically, but not always) incorporated within the established device. In other cases, a new peripheral device (to borrow an item of computer terminology) is added. An example of such a new peripheral is the telephone answering machine, which enables callers to leave messages, and is usually an additional device, incorporating a tape recorder, that sits alongside the conventional telephone.

It is possible to list many new functions that are being added to items of household equipment: but there are several difficulties in providing a systematic account of them. One problem is in defining which functions are being added to which devices: is a wristwatch with calculator, diary and address book functions really an augmented wristwatch—or is it a portable calculator with accessories? The supplier's answer may be more a matter of marketing strategy (or industry of origin) than of technical characteristics.

Another problem is that it is often in practice difficult to draw a firm boundary between improvements in existing functions and the addition of radically new functions. Take, for example, the addition of an electronic clock/timer to a device that previously might have featured an electronic or electromechanical one. Here there may not appear to be any real addition of new functions. But in many such cases manufacturers are capitalising on microprocessor control in order to increase the programmability of equipment, when previously only a few fixed options were provided. To decide on whether or not new functions are being added in many such borderline cases requires determining the details of the change in function; for example, is the timer now able to control the appliance in new ways, heretofore impossible? How far does programmability go beyond selection of preset options?

As the last example suggests, in many cases the substitution of micro-electronic for electronic, electromechanical, or even mechanical devices provides the basis for new functions. Consider another example, that of the CD player, which at first sight substitutes for the conventional record player, and merely improves upon it in terms of sound quality and size. But, in addition, new levels of programmability are available: the player can be instructed to repeat, search for or skip certain tracks, for example—and such features are available in mass market systems, not merely as extras in the top-of-the-range models. (And, as in the past mature technologies have often been stimulated into a new wave of innovation by competitive challenges from radical new technologies, so the conventional record player now appears to be the focus of more innovative effort.) For another example, the typical digital wristwatch offers an alarm, a timer, a calendar, and often other functions, as standard features. (Again, this has promoted a surge of competitive innovation in conventional watches.)

It seems likely that the innovation process, adding new functions to both the CD player and the electronic wristwatch, has much further to run. Many of these functions will probably remain forever beyond the reach of the conventional technologies. Thus, portable personal stereo CD players are already available (they can be carried on one's belt or in a pocket, and provide ample output to power headphones), and some CD players are already provided with output sockets which will enable them to be linked directly to forthcoming generations of digital amplifiers and recorders. We can say with some confidence that conventional record players will not be given these characteristics.

Likewise, it is already common to see digital watches which incorporate calculators and memory to be used for minimal diaries or phone lists, and we have seen wrist computers/terminals being marketed that include (retain?) watch functions but go so far beyond these as to be quite novel devices. For example, the Psion Organiser II is promoted as being simultaneously: a clock and calendar; a diary with alarm facilities; eight alarm clocks; an indexed filing cabinet; a smart calculator; and a menu-driven computer. Extra plug-in programmes include financial analysis, money management, mathematical analysis, spelling checkers, etc., and business applications include bar code and magnetic card readers as well as communications facilities to electronic mail or other computers (Psion, 1986).

Whatever the difficulties in deciding whether specific innovations represent the addition of new functions to equipment or the introduction of new products, we can at least go *some* way towards understanding the nature of these innovations. Four facets of the application of IT to household products contribute to the development of new functions. These are:

— the development of digital controls and displays in all types of device;
— the use of microprocessors in the central operating processes of audio and video equipment;
— the rapid lowering of RAM memory costs, so that information can be stored by equipment;
— and the addition of communications input/output interfaces to equipment.

It is almost inevitable that these features of HI will be used in order to lead to a proliferation of new functions. Indeed, this is such an elementary step that many innovations of this sort represent little more than unnecessary gimmicks. (For instance, how many LED clocks does one really need in a room?) Some of the new functions—perhaps particularly those displayed on portable devices like wristwatches—may be status symbols, whose main 'informational function' is to demonstrate the owner's wealth, taste or infatuation with hi-tech. But a number of utilitarian functions are already being marketed or are under development and likely to emerge in the near future.

Such utilitarian functions, and applications of these, are outlined in Table 2.5. But, in addition to the discussion above, it should be pointed out that the development of household appliances, and especially the addition of new functions to equipment, is being driven along by more than just the application of IT to consumer goods. For example, one aspect of current product differentiation, reinforced by IT capabilities, but also reflecting social trends, is the development of smaller and more portable devices. In some cases, such as countertop dishwashers and mini-ovens, the main driving force seems to be the recognition of a market opportunity based on the increasing number of small, single-person households. Other instances, such as personal stereo systems, and some cordless devices (those that involve data transmission—others are based on battery power) do benefit from the small-scale (and low-power consumption) of microelectronics. Whatever the driving force, it is apparent that many devices are becoming available in a wider variety of sizes, and are being made more portable in other ways—to the extent of radios which can be for use in the shower, cameras that can be taken swimming. One consequence of this tendency may be the dissemination of several varieties of the same item around households: it is not at all uncommon to find multi-car, multi-TV, multi-music centre families, for example. If flexible manufacturing does permit wider product differentiation, such a trend may well be intensified.

Table 2.5 New functions being added to household goods

— *Memories*. Telephones, for example, have had answering machines added, so that they can receive and store messages when the owner is unavailable; and new phones can 'dial' frequently required numbers in response to a few keypresses (and, in products being developed, on the basis of a voice input).

— *Safety features*. Examples of these are warning indicators and alarms that indicate that, for example, a refrigerator's power supplies have been interrupted, the device is overloaded, or something appears to be amiss (blockages, burning, etc.); and simple triggers that turn off devices when they appear to be malfunctioning (e.g. when gas is not ignited). Automobiles are being equipped with such features to provide feedback to drivers — or even to disable the car — when seat belts are not fastened, speed limits are exceeded, or some threshold has been exceeded (e.g. low oil levels, or, as in a system on trial for alcohol abusers in the United States, high driver alcohol levels), etc.

— *Maintenance features*. These have perhaps been pioneered in the office environment by manufacturers of such items as photocopying machines, which have installed displays that inform users where a paper jam has occurred or what they need to do (add ink, toner, etc.) if copies are inadequate. Some automobiles are fitted with internal monitoring systems that allow garages to quickly establish the source of problems: with lowered microcomputer costs, these diagnostics could be performed automatically by the car itself. Such auto-diagnostic displays, perhaps indicating not only where the probable locus of a problem is, but also what steps should be taken to overcome it, could be installed on many durables.

— *Energy conservation features*. Again, innovation in automobiles prefigures developments that are emerging or foreseeable in many consumer goods. A considerable increase in the energy efficiency of motors has been achieved by regulating their fuel consumption and performance by microelectronic controls. Similar innovations may be applied to other energy-intensive goods, such as washing machines and dryers. In addition, energy conservation may be served by the provision of more information to users of the energy costs of particular operating choices ('What will the effect on the fuel bill be of choosing to keep this room one degree warmer?'), and the ability of microprocessor controls to be linked to sensors or communications systems in order to adjust their operations according to environmental changes (e.g. time of day, temperature rise), or to signals received from remote or distant sources (e.g. concerning changes in energy tariff rates or TV programming).

— *Communications*. The addition of communications features can enhance each of the improved functions noted above. For example, prototype devices (some in use in advanced business installations) can transmit their emergency alarms by telephone, adjust their operations according to signals about electricity tariff rates transmitted together with their power supply, and be interrogated remotely about the reasons for their apparent malfunctioning.

2.4 New household products

A third class of development, again overlapping with the innovation trajectories discussed previously, involves *new household products* using IT. Several now-familiar devices and services which we have already discussed may well be regarded as new products:

— microwave cookers;
— CD players;
— videotape recorders and cameras;
— viewdata;
— home computers (and their peripherals);
— video games, etc.

Other products that we have mentioned are well under development:

— new CD systems such as CD-I;
— High Definition TV, flat TV;
— 'smart' alarms and meters;
— new ISDN-based telecommunications services;
— health monitoring systems, etc.

There is some difficulty in classifying what are new products as compared to what are simply improved products. One useful approach to defining 'new products' is to refer to those household goods and services that either permit households to undertake new activities, or that promote major change in the way in which household activities are carried out. But whether or not there are really any substantially new activities taking place in the household is very much a matter of definition. If we formulate activities in very specific ways (e.g. watching TV, using a washing machine), then we will be able to identify many new activities. But, from a more general viewpoint, there are few, if any, additions to the familiar household functions such as childcare, entertainment, social and sexual intercourse, personal care, etc.

There are, however, also transfers of activities between the formal economy and the household. Historically, for example, many of what at least the less benighted parts of industrial society accept as basic Welfare State provisions were formerly left to families or small communities to supply to the best of their ability. Social historians often describe the growth of the Welfare State as involving a shift of activities and responsibilities from the household to the state. But, in the last few decades, many activities have also been transferred from the formal economy to the household.

These latter transfers have often been associated with the introduction of new household technologies which permit functions formerly supplied by traditional services to be achieved in new ways. Over the post-war decades, cheap motor power (petrol engines and electric motors) and electronics (valve and transistor-based systems) enabled households to evade the economies of scale in the production and delivery of services which previously underpinned the use of facilities like laundries, cinemas and public transport utilities.[7]

Before considering whether IT might further such trends, let us examine these examples a little further. The motor car and the washing machine are used to provide services for consumers— transport and cleaning in these cases—that might otherwise be purchased as final services from the formal economy (e.g. by riding on a bus or sending washing to a laundry). The 'self-service' mode of provision involved here may not involve any radically new household goals, but does require informal labour inputs to the core task. But some other household technologies call for very little (if any) labour input: watching TV, for example, may even require less effort than going out to the cinema. Thus they are not so much 'self-services' as a shift from a traditional mode of service provision to one based on new technological systems (both in the service organisations themselves, for example broadcasting, and in the household, for example TV sets).

Two aspects of these new modes of service provision are significant: first, some new skills may be required to use the technologies (minimal in some cases, but in others—'self-services' such as car driving, for example—of a relatively high level). These skills may occasion new household goals and divisions of labour. Second, changes in the cost and effort associated with activities may change the final functions to which these are directed: motoring may itself become a pleasure activity ('cruising'), watching TV lacks the socialising that theatres traditionally provided, for instance.

There is a fuzzy boundary between a new product, as we have defined it above, and what is simply a considerably improved version of an existing product. Our approach has not been so much based on the technical methods employed (e.g. whether audio material is recorded in analogue or digital form), but in terms of the change in activities that may be associated with the new product. For example, the microwave cooker involves a new way of carrying out the core function of cooking, and by altering the characteristics of the process, has led to some shift in activity. It seems that new patterns of family dining are emerging around the microwave cooker, since it becomes much easier to rapidly cook a convenience or pre-prepared meal; this means that men are more prepared to take up some cooking activities, and that individual members of families are eating at their own convenience rather than communally—though 'mother' often remains responsible for the original meal planning and preparation.

The extent to which a qualitative change in activities may be associated with HI will depend upon the degree to which the new technology's design characteristics differ from that for which it is substituting. Key characteristics, for example, will include: costs, improvements in convenience (portability, skills required), and the variety of new functions provided. When a new device removes the need for relatively laborious or skilled physical or intellectual labour, the change in activities may be very marked: since the potential user base is increased, the time involved may well be reduced, the possibility of carrying out several activities at once grows, drudgery may become fun or a skilled task may be routinised, and so on. Such major changes in activities may well be a consequence of home computers and computer-communications, for example.

The development of HI, based on low-cost to massive volumes of information and data-processing power, is liable to lead to the 'informatisation' of many current household activities; that is, the largely unrecognised work of planning stages of an activity, and testing out expectations against perceptions, which are involved in even the most mundane household activities, will often be augmented by IT. This is liable to promote substantial changes in a wide range of activities, with an even wider range of activities changing less markedly (e.g. with improvements in the quality of performance of the activities or the ability of relatively unskilled people to engage in them). On this last point, for example, it could be argued that many men's readiness to use convenience foods and microwave ovens reflects their perception that they will not need to acquire difficult and/or 'feminine' skills to use them.

Improved controls and outputs, especially in so far as these simplify tasks or ensure higher levels of quality control, will certainly contribute to this process. In addition, the provision of information from external databases or from domestic mass data storage could be applied to various household activities. Examples of this might be: personal transport (e.g. trip planning), cooking (e.g. menu planning, recipes), the efficient use of energy (e.g. matching use of devices and the opening/closing of windows and doors to energy costs), shopping (consumer advice and product specifications), and some forms of entertainment (broadcasting schedules, hints and tips for games). Data might be accessed via new telephone services, broadcast teletext, narrowcast cable TV services, online computer communications and viewdata, CD-I systems, and other technical modes of delivery. Likely developments here, then, are online and broadcast data services (building on current dial-a-menu and traffic/weather news) and the incorporation of 'cookery books' and 'home maintenance manuals' into household appliances and into new types of home information centre.

Finally, we should note that familiar devices may effectively become 'new products' if changes in their cost or capabilities means that they can be applied to functions very different from those to which we are accustomed. One example will suffice: the flat-screen, enlarged VDU. When such devices become available, it is quite plausible that the home VDU will no longer be mainly used for TV viewing. 'Wallpaper' TV can still be displayed through it; but so can other material, including, perhaps, something rather more like wallpaper, or like other indoor decorations. If the VDU is hanging on the wall all the time, why not use it to display still or moving graphics: maybe new art forms will be developed for it? An improved product may, as this example indicates, become a new product, if its new functions come to displace its original role.

2.5 The integration of equipment

Our fourth, and last, general development in household technology was the *integration of equipment*. We have long been aware of tendencies to put different devices together, often in one box—ranging from the integrated music centre to the simple combination of a clock and radio in the same housing. The use of microelectronics and digital controls makes it more feasible to consider relating together the operation of devices that are in the same box (so that the clock, for example, can be used to turn on the radio). But it also increases the utility of interrelating devices that are not in the same box, by getting them to communicate with each other through the home. Such a trajectory moves towards what is often known as 'home automation': in the United States and Japan the term 'smart house' has some popularity, while in Western Europe the phrase 'Interactive Home Systems' conveys much the same image.

'Home automation' may carry connotations of office automation as it is taking place in the formal economy, and indeed there is a transfer of ideas and techniques from the 'smart building'—an office environment that is still in a relatively immature stage of development. But 'automation' also conjures up the image of the automated factory; this is quite innappropriate, since the control of household equipment along the lines of factory robotics and assembly line technology will probably remain prohibitively expensive for general-purpose domestic use in the immediate future. (There may be applications in special instances, however; for example, for disabled people.) However, linkage of a wide range of household devices through a 'homenet' or 'Small Area Network', the domestic equivalent of the 'Local Area Network' in business, could permit automation to the extent that devices are electronically controlled by changes in their own state or that of other devices or the environment, so that previous requirements for human decision-making and labour are substantially reduced.

Scepticism about HI reaches a peak where ideas of the smart house are discussed. And, indeed, there does seem to be some contradiction between the decreased cost and increased portablity of equipment and the idea of integrating it. Why have audio relayed from room to room (as traditional hi-fi enthusiasts would do) when a music centre can be carried around, or several systems installed around the house? However, HI allows for more than the relatively passive relaying of signals from a source room to a destination—it permits interactivity of devices. This means that it has considerably wider appeal than the hi-fi enthusiast example suggests.

In some instances, the rationale for integrating equipment may be con-venience—the classic example being that of being able to follow the same recording while one is moving around the house, for example, without depriving those who are remaining stationary, is certainly one example of this. But so too are in—home communications systems (e.g. being able to 'telephone' someone who is in a distant part of the garden, being able to check that the baby is asleep). In some cases the rationale may be based more on security concerns: having the ability to monitor the state of the house from one's workplace, for example, or to see who is at the front door while staying in the sitting room. And in other cases it may be based on automation, going beyond simply being able to unlock the front door remotely to, for example, using 'informed equipment', such as the 'smart meters' that are capable of sending signals to other items of equipment to inform them that tariff rates have changed (so that, if they have been programmed to operate only in a low-cost energy mode, they should turn on or off).

There seem to be many circumstances under which the integration of equipment might be promoted. Whether this takes the form of specific items being related together, or of a more comprehensive 'smart house' system, will depend on these circumstances, together with issues such as the cost of equipment and of installing home communications systems. We shall devote more attention to the development of intercommunicating and integrated home applications of IT in later chapters. In terms of product and market development strategies, and of potential areas of consumer demand.

Notes

1. For recent examples of such trend projections see Miles, Rush, Turner and Bessant (1988 forthcoming), and the October 1987 issue of *Scientific American*.
2. On the notions of 'heartland technology' and an analysis of the implications of change in such technology, see Freeman, Clark and Soete (1982); Perez (1983, 1985).
3. The interactive touch-sensitive display system in question is the result of collaborative development by Phosphor Products Company Limited and Tube Investments Research Laboratories. Its graphics are displayed on a 640 × 256 pixels display which accomodates 128 distinct touch switches in a 16 × 8 array (Phosphor Products, 1986). Reference to specific products in the text does not constitute endorsement of them.
4. Many examples of prototype and experimental items of domestic equipment of this sort are provided in the May 1985 issue of *IEEE Spectrum*, which has been a very useful source for this discussion, and is a good starting-point for further reading about HI innovations.
5. We here draw on Turner (1986a, b) and Philips (1986). It should be noted that there has been some controversy over the similarities and differences between CD-=I and CD-ROM, which (as was pointed out by *CD-I News*, 1986) reflects market strategies as well as technical specifications: some commentators object to the identification of CD-I as a distinct type of system. For a useful tabulation of features of emerging CD-type systems, see the January 1988 issue of the magazine *CD-ROM*.
6. This use of 'teleport' to describe a videophone should not be confused with either the science-fictional concept of matter transmission, or its recent and now rather

more common application to data communications centres established as facilities for urban areas.

7. See Gershuny and Miles (1983) for an analysis of data, from a number of Western European economies, depicting the shift of various functions from service sectors of the formal economy to forms of production and consumption activity within the household. This 1983 book builds on the early pioneering work of Gershuny (1977) on 'self-services'.

3 Innovation and diffusion in Home Informatics

3.1 Captain Midnight's children

'Captain Midnight' was practically a popular hero among North American consumers in April 1986. Over a million households had put up satellite dishes on or near their houses to receive DBS television—in particular to intercept the programmes sent to cable TV (CATV) distributors, without having to pay for CATV (though having paid perhaps $1000 for their dishes). The cable operators, beginning with Home Box Office, retaliated: 'they "scrambled" the audio and video signals, so that they could only be decrypted by CATV distributors, or by households buying a decoder plus access to the programming'.

Captain Midnight struck back as the cable operators' actions began to bite. He 'hacked' into the TV transmissions, lambasting the companies for what he saw as outrageous charges. And well might he see them as such, for he was a dish dealer: satellite dish sales had dropped catastrophically in the few months after scrambling started, and many dealers were going out of business. Captain Midnight was eventually identified and prosecuted, but political pressure from dish owners was intense. The US Senate instituted hearings on whether dish owners were being overcharged as compared to CATV subscribers (an equity issue was at stake—many rural users had no access to cable). Pirate decoders began to appear on the market, and the broadcasters were forced to change their systems; new generation pirate decoders are now being developed, according to journalistic sources.

Why dwell on this story? The reason is that this is a perfect illustration of the complex nature of what is generally referred to as the 'diffusion process'. The incident highlights:

— the relation between consumer purchase of hardware and their expectations of being able to obtain software (in this case TV programmes) at a reasonable price (in this case free);
— the use of technological innovations to exploit facilities in ways unanticipated by service providers (private dishes to receive transmissions intended for CATV—though some see the cable operators as hoping to establish captive audiences!);
— the appearance of counter-innovations (pirate decoders);
— the translation of consumer concerns into political pressures, pursued by both orthodox means (lobbying) and unorthodox ones which use the new technology (hacking).

And our account above, it must be admitted, is a highly simplified one: it has made no mention of the interplay between analogue and digital technologies, of the borrowing of encryption techniques from military computer communications, of the cable operators' realisation that they could not only use decoders themselves, but also market them as consumer goods. . . .

Similar issues are raised in many other areas of HI. Home computers, for example, have been the stimulus to the formation of many 'computer clubs'. And a major function of these clubs has been the exchange of pirated software, and of the skills needed to break the protection that software authors build into their programmes. Many home computer users might not have acquired their machines had they not believed that they would be able to acquire lots of software at low cost; but also in this case, unlike the DBS users, the busting of software protection was certainly part of the pleasure, perhaps the main pleasure, for a not insignificant proportion of users.[1]

The interplay between pirates (often children and adolescents, but sometimes unscrupulous dealers) and producers must have been one of the most skill-enhancing contests of all time; but, recognising that practically any protection will sooner or later be rendered vulnerable to a new 'Copy-All' programme, publishers of both games and commercial software have been moving towards alternatives to software protection. One approach is to build much necessary information into the manual, and perhaps also to make the manual difficult to photocopy. Another is to make the programme available as 'shareware', distributed freely but with the request that satisfied users make a contribution: the hope here is that a much larger market will be accessed, and that users will be more inclined to make a donation to 'cover costs' than to pay the inflated prices of much commercial software.

Piracy is a topic that crops up frequently: it is currently a lively issue in debates about Digital Audio Tape, where it is a threat that is being used to justify pleas for product design of particular kinds. It is prominent in part because IT means that information can be reproduced extremely cheaply (recall Table 2.1) and there thus appears a considerable disparity (one or even two orders of magnitude) between the cost of purchase of the genuine item and the cost of running off a pirate copy. But it is only one of a number of phenomena that underline the point that diffusion is a complex process, and in some ways is one of the least interesting of them; for all it really involves is consumers attempting to get more of the project without paying for it (or distributors being able to sell it without paying the full rate for it), while product innovation seeks to exploit this (pirate decoders, 'Copy-All') or avert it (better encryption and protection). Many other features of the diffusion process also involve an interplay between the shaping of the form of the product and the evolution of the consumer market, however.

One problem here is that the study of innovation and diffusion has been somewhat dominated by empirical analyses of innovation in intermediate goods. Thus there has been considerable research into such topics as the behaviour of firms acquiring process innovations and that of farmers using

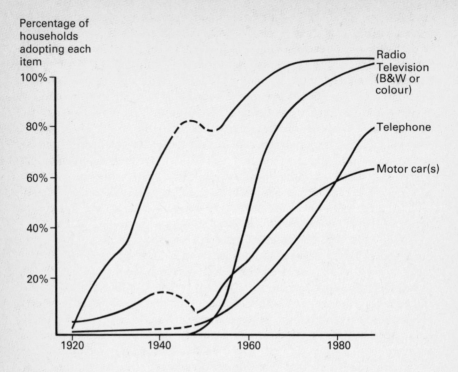

Figure 3.1   The diffusion of consumer goods: selected examples in the United Kingdom

Source: Various issues of *Social Trends*, and Hendry (1972)

new crops or fertilisers. Some of the main features described in such studies do also apply to the diffusion of new consumer technologies. Perhaps most notable among these is the applicability of the logistic or S-curve, providing a more or less accurate description of the take-up of a successful new product or process in a population, to the diffusion of consumer and producer goods alike. (We shall discuss this 'model' of the diffusion process shortly.) But there are also points of divergence in the motivations of producers in the formal economy and those of households (even though these may well be producers in the informal economy), and we shall need to consider some of these similarities and differences.

3.2 The diffusion process: behind the logistic curve

Some of the early literature on the diffusion of innovations portrayed the process as a simple affair that could readily be depicted in terms of mathematical graphs. The innovation itself was portrayed as an all-or-nothing thing, as if the technology acquired by early and late adopters was identical; adoption of an innovation was implicitly treated as a good thing, with early adopters being well-informed and late adopters being ignorant or isolated from communications networks; and the spread of the innovation was essentially a matter of increasing numbers of potential users who were becoming aware of or convinced of the potential of the technology for their own purposes. Figure 3.1 displays displays British data on the diffusion of various consumer technologies whose uptake has more or less roughly approximated a logistic curve.

But, for several decades now, at least, more sophisticated studies of industrial innovation have been underlining the point that diffusion is not simply a mechanical process like the diffusion of a dye in water or a vapour in air. Nor does it correspond to a simple biological model, say one where a virus invades a non-resistant organism or a passive environment accepts a species from outside. For some authors, the situation is much more like an ecological one, where environment and species co-evolve; but perhaps it is more complex still, since human consciousness is involved on the part of change agents and users of technology.[2]

Figure 3.2 draws on the results of diffusion studies to present what necessarily is a rather exaggerated view of some of the main characteristics of both adopters of innovations and of the innovations themselves. It is exaggerated, in that the features outlined are by no means always as clear-cut as suggested here, the S-curve of diffusion is often by no means as smooth or symmetrical as implied, and, of course, some innovations are simply failures and never achieve the take-off after finding early adopters (indeed, some never even find early adopters!). The diffusion literature also goes on to identify a stage of product decline, when the innovation is substituted for by new technologies, or rendered obsolete by social changes.

The industrial innovation literature points out that, far from being passive receivers of messages about innovations, potential adopters of a new product or technique are involved in a learning and decision-making process. They often actively seek information about the technology; they weigh up various considerations (cost, usefulness, ease of use, life-span, etc.) in order to make the choice of whether or not to use it. And if the decision is made in favour of adoption, the learning process still continues. The actors may need to, or rather, may find it is in their interests to:

— change their working practices so as to make efficient and effective use of the technology;
— revise their preparations for these practices (e.g. recruitment and training);
— and, perhaps, restructure the organisational arrangements that organise it (e.g. the division of labour, systems of management and supervision).

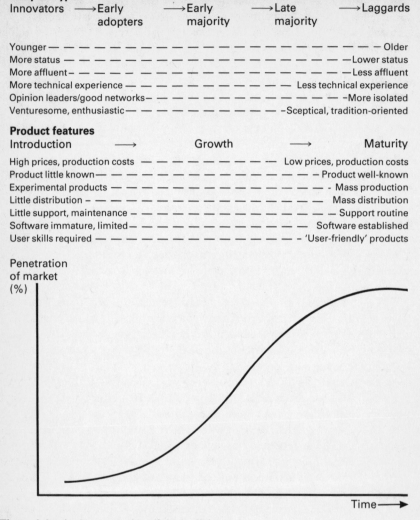

Adopter types

| Innovators | →Early adopters | →Early majority | →Late majority | →Laggards |

| Younger — Older |
| More status —Lower status |
| More affluent —Less affluent |
| More technical experience — — — — — — — — — — — Less technical experience |
| Opinion leaders/good networks— — — — — — — — — — — — — — — -More isolated |
| Venturesome, enthusiastic— — — — — — — — — — — -Sceptical, tradition-oriented |

Product features

| Introduction | ⟶ | Growth | ⟶ | Maturity |

| High prices, production costs — — — — — — — — — Low prices, production costs |
| Product little known— — — — — — — — — — — — — — — — — — Product well-known |
| Experimental products — — — — — — — — — — — — — — — — — - Mass production |
| Little distribution - — — — — — — — — — — — — — — — — — — Mass distribution |
| Little support, maintenance - — — — — — — — — — — — — — — — Support routine |
| Software immature, limited— — — — — — — — — — — — — — Software established |
| User skills required — — — — — — — — — — — — — — — - 'User-friendly' products |

Penetration
of market
(%)

Time⟶

Figure 3.2   An interpretation of the logistic curve

Sources: Based on numerous surveys of diffusion research, especially Poill (1968) and Rogers (1962).

As time elapses they acquire skills in the use of the technology, and they may implement further innovations or modify the technology to make it more appropriate to their specific requirements.

Especially when it comes to purchases of expensive items of equipment, households resemble firms in many of these respects—for example, engaging in 'search behaviour' by inspecting alternatives in shops, catalogues, consumer magazines, friends' houses, etc. It may be that private households rarely institute training programmes—although one can think of cookery classes and driving lessons—but there are other preparations made before engaging in informal work and leisure activities (e.g. packing to go on a picnic). And the organisational arrangements of households are typically far less formalised than those of firms; but there are informal arrangements that may well be altered quite dramatically (as in the preparation and consumption of microwave- as compared to oven-cooked food).

Of course, consumers may be more likely than firms to engage in 'impulse buying' of relatively cheap items. What is more, non-durables are themselves often the object of immediate consumption, whereas consumer durables are often used for productive purposes (in the informal economy) and thus resemble intermediate goods. (This is far from a hard-and-fast rule: the TV is an entertainment good; detergents are non-durables!)

Thus, even while the origins of household devices typically lie in the formal economy—households do not carry out extensive R&D programmes as a rule!—the consumer technology diffusion process is an active one. This point has been taken up by few of the very few commentators who have addressed the issue of HI. One exception here is the work of Vitalari and Venkatesh (1987), whose view of the likely path of development of 'in-home computing and information services' is summarised in Table 3.1. Their work does take into account the need for factors such as telecommunications infrastructure, training and computer literacy, maintenance and support, security and legal safeguards and standards in the evolution of HI. These authors expect exposure to computers and advances in rendering new technologies appropriate for household use to interact positively so as to yield a logistic curve-type diffusion of HI, which they describe in terms of a number of stages, as depicted in Table 3.1. Nevertheless, they do also indicate the possibilities for consolidation of 'information-poor' groups, and are not altogether reassuring about the political and psychological implications of their scenario.

The Vitalari and Venkatesh approach is based on analogies with the diffusion of earlier consumer goods. But not all new technologies have taken off in this way, of course, although others—TV, telephones, motor cars, etc.—have. Is it reasonable to project this sort of success for HI?

Some light may be shed on this by considering previous successes and failures in consumer innovation. Consider, for example, earlier communications technolgies. 'Ham', amateur radio never really got beyond the hobbyist stage to mass usage. Easy-to-use telephones make it far easier for users to get in contact with the person they are actually seeking. Citizen's Band radio has more recently been more successful, in part because it is now more user-friendly and portable, so it can be applied by people on the move who are less concerned with making contact with a known person than with relating to a community—e.g. truckers sharing details of traffic problems.

Are new home information systems fated to follow the course of amateur radio, or that of telephones and TV? Whatever the merits of Vitalari and

Table 3.1   Vitalari–Venkatesh model of the progress of HI

Stage	Features
1975–79 Hobby/expert (HPL < 1%)	First personal computers, hobbyists
1980–84 Home entertainment (HPL 10%)	Growing sales of PCs, beginnings of computer subculture
1985–89 Multifunction (HPL 20%)	Service providers assess home markets, market segmentation, computers used for self-advancement, minor problems of juvenile crime (hacking).
1990–94 Service/information utility (HPL 30%)	Emergence of information subcultures, information poor; work-at-home; white-collar crime; electronic opinion and political polling.
1995–99 Robotics/home control (HPL 40%)	Worldwide information trade, automated monitoring systems impact services, demise of broadcast presentation mode; new political constituencies formed.
2000+ Household appliance (HPL 60%)	Information industry dominant sector in United States, reinstitutionalisation of household, social impact of information subcultures.

Note: HPL = Household Penetration Level

Source: Based on Tables 2 and 3 of Vitalari and Venkatesh (1987), with some reorganisation, many omissions (this is really a set of highlights from their account), and some rephrasing of terminology.

Venkatesh's detailed forecasts, we would agree that the latter is more likely. For reasons already indicated in Chapter 2 (e.g. Figure 2.2), HI offers consumers considerable advantages, and the basic technology is so malleable that it is overwhelmingly likely that applications which appeal to wide markets will be identified and developed. IT is a technological revolution, and just as some electronics technologies were bound to find success (whether these were amateur radio or telephones), so will some microelectronics. However, the way in which HI does emerge in the home may not involve manifestations that users will automatically label 'home computers' or 'information systems'. Instead, as will be suggested in Chapter 5, the pattern of development could quite plausibly be less in terms of suppliers marketing technologies as such, and more in terms of their providing specific, appealing applications: less a matter of devices and more a matter of services delivered.

The next two sections will take up two facets of the active nature of the diffusion process. First, consumers are not simply a passive environment into which new products spread; and, second, the use of a new product is much more than a reflexive adaptation of consumer habits and lifestyles to a new technology.

3.3 Diffusion as an active process

Like business purchasers, private individuals are actively making decisions about which products to acquire. There are marked differences between individuals and socioeconomic groups, and in orientations to different classes of products. Nevertheless, in general we can say that, while many buying decisions are essentially habitual ones, where new products are concerned (especially durables) consumers pay attention to information about the characteristics of competing products. The information that is sought on products includes:

— how much they cost;
— how well they are likely to perform;
— what are likely future trends in costs and performance;
— what will incidental and repair costs be;
— how far will complementary services and necessary software be available now and in the future.

A series of theoretical and empirical investigations recently carried out for a programme of research into 'Public Acceptance of New Technologies'[3] underline these points. To summarise some of the conclusions reached here, consumers, like industrial purchasers of new technologies, often display caution in making investments into what are perceived as immature technologies. If standards are perceived as being in flux, so that complementary services (for example those like broadcasting or recording that supply data inputs for electronic devices) may be unavailable in the future, or if the model is liable to become obsolete so that spare parts and repair services may be unavailable, then there are deterrents to purchase. Awareness of these problems may be particularly high in a period of rapid change and many competing new products: a recent example was the competition between several VTR systems (V2000, VHS, Betamax, and, in addition, the competition between VTRs and videodiscs), which has led to some early purchasers acquiring equipment of relatively restricted usefulness. (The second-hand prices for the non-standard systems are depressed well below those of the successful ones, a clear indicator of consumers' negative appraisal of their usefulness.)

Such deterrents may be overwhelmed by the perception of strong immediate advantages of equipment; or by the perception of 'future proofing' of equipment such that it should be adaptable to what standards eventually emerge (which requires consumers to evaluate the reliability of manufacturers' claims). While a minority of consumers are keen experimenters (located before the 'take-off' of the S-curve), more are cautious, preferring to wait until they have had an opportunity to satisfy themselves that the devices will and will continue to fulfil their claims, and that without becoming rapidly obsolete or unusable (there consumers will be on the rapidly accelerating portion of the S-curve). The 'Public Acceptance of New Technologies' report argued, in the light of such considerations, that Britain's system of TV rentals has allowed consumers to engage in low-risk experimentation (and for reducing costs by selling-off ex-rental items at low prices), and thus encouraged a relatively high rate of diffusion of TV-related innovations — teletext, video recorders, infra-red remote controls, and colour TV itself.

A sense of rapid change in the sphere of consumer technologies may, then, actually mitigate against the take-up of new devices: consumers may prefer to wait until the virtues of competing designs are more clearly evident, or until mass production has substantially reduced costs to an apparently stable level. It is this sense of rapid change that the 'In Three Years, TV as We Know It will Cease to Exist' advertisement cited at the beginning of this book is attempting to foster, of course — in this case in order to create mild alarm and steer the market towards rental rather than purchase.

Public political disagreements over standards (for example, the dispute between North America and Japan on the one hand, and Europe on the other, concerning transmission standards for widescreen and high-definition TV systems) may also increase uncertainly about future support for new systems, and thus lessen consumer adoption of the new technology. How serious these problems are will depend on the degree to which an immediate decision is seen to yield immediate benefits: thus the rapid success of CD and VTR systems, and (perhaps) the more mixed reception awarded to home computers (where problems of incompatibility were particularly strong, while usefulness was less apparent).

The problem of 'future proofing' is a subset of a number of more general problems referred to as the issues of forward and backward (reverse) compatibility. These two terms refer to the questions:

— will this piece of equipment work with the services that will be standard in the future? For example, if I purchase the currently available TV set, will I be able to watch future broadcasts, even if I cannot appreciate all of their quality without a new investment? (Thus, monochrome TVs can receive colour transmissions, even if they cannot display the colours.)
— does this piece of equipment make the most of services that were standard for previous generations of equipment? For example, if I

purchase a new type of TV, will I be able to watch conventional broadcasts? (Thus, colour TVs can receive monochrome broadcasts.)

In recent business purchasing decisions, these problems have been particularly acute and prominent with respect to computer software, giving rise to the *de facto* IBM standard being adopted by a majority of microcomputer purchasers. But the problems apply very generally to consumer goods too, in some cases involving the complementary services that allow the goods to be made full use of, in some cases involving semi-durables and perishable items that satisfy these requirements (e.g. detergents suitable for use in new washing machines, convenience foods packaged so that they can be used in microwave ovens). In studies of industrial innovation, the point has been made that technological trajectories involve the formation of a social network involving suppliers and users.[4] The same can be argued for consumer product innovation. Except in a few simple cases, major consumer product innovation typically requires not just a single new good or service, but a whole system of interrelated innovations—manufacturers, distributors, suppliers of complementary services, regulators, consumer bodies, etc.

The creation of such a system necessarily requires some considerable time and effort. But when an existing range of products is modified or enlarged then the innovation process involves modifications in a given system rather than the construction of a system from scratch. This may also apply to dramatic product innovations that build upon existing consumer activities and services. Radio and television were able to draw upon existing networks of journalists and actors, for example, even if new retail outlets and engineering skills were also required for the products' success. The microwave cooker is an example where existing retail outlets could be exploited and where complementary goods and services already existed. (Thus, while new convenience foods and cooking utensils appropriate to microwave cooking have been introduced, many existing foodstuffs and utensils could already be used.)

But other radical new products may pose the requirement of constructing a new system and many of its elements. Sometimes the problems are resolved by regulation or informal agreement: thus the effort to assure that viewdata/videotex and teletext systems used the same format, and that changes in TV broadcast systems have been gradual and where possible have allowed for both forms of compatibility. On other occasions the problems are more acute, and part of the explanation for the disappointments associated with consumer use of viewdata in most Western countries may lie in the difficulties that these countries faced in establishing an appropriate system of innovations and innovators. One of the issues that we shall confront in Chapter 5 is the strategic choice faced by the producers of new consumer technologies as to whether to build on existing systems in an incremental way, or whether to go for 'quantum leaps', hoping that the advantages of a radical step in technological performance will outweigh the absence of an established system of interrelated social and technological innovations—and lead to the rapid establishment of the appropriate networks, support structures, etc.

3.4 Social innovations

The adoption process is, we have emphasised, a more active one than the term 'diffusion' implies. What about the use of new products? In the case of industrial innovation, researchers have stressed the active nature of the implementation of new process technologies: firms modify the technologies themselves (much unrecorded innovation takes place in the office and on the shopfloor), and it is often found that greater gains can be achieved from them from technological innovations by reorganising working practices and relationships.

Rather similar phenomena occur in the consumer use of technologies, even if the reworking of consumer products may be rather less frequent and systematic than that involved in the formal economy. In the informal economy, products may be used in unexpected ways (for example, viewdata services have proved to be especially popular for messaging rather than as a means to consult databases), and they may be modified by consumers (although this may be more often true for mechanical hardware and, perhaps, software, than for electronic devices).

Often, too, the use of new products is associated with substantial changes in people's ways of life: the microwave cooker, for example, is associated with considerable shifts in family food preparation and eating habits (e.g. more men cooking convenience meals, a move towards individual rather than family meals). Consider the changes associated with the motor car: it rapidly began to be used not just as a preferred means of transport for established journeys, but it also became the focus for new pleasure trips, and led to a reshaping of social interactions (it is often claimed that the teenage sexual practices of post-war years were substantially affected by the availability of mobile privacy and comfort), and to reorganising living patterns (suburban dwelling, supermarket shopping). New living patterns were established, with the move to suburbia. Often the full benefits of a new product such as the automobile are only reaped when such innovations in ways of life are undertaken, and when the complementary services (e.g. supermarkets in appropriate locations and with parking facilities) and infrastructures (good motorways) are established.

Indeed, without people's willingness to create changes in their ways of life (and often in the ways of life of others that are associated with them!)—in other words, to be innovative in their patterns of production and consumption in the informal economy as well as the formal economy—there would be no final demand for technologically innovative products, other than for minor improvements of existing applications.

Thus, the learning process is not merely a reflexive adaptation of human behaviour to a given technology. But we should also note that technologies themselves are modified by the development of their uses, as manufacturers and providers of complementary services and infrastructure learn what characteristics of the new products are particularly desired, and redesign the products to fit emerging market niches. Again, this is a point that has been well-documented in respect of intermediate goods: while links between suppliers and users are typically less direct in the consumer sphere, market signals and market research play a similar role here.

This brings us to the longstanding debate in innovation research between 'technology-push' and 'demand-pull' theories of innovation. The former essentially argues that product innovations derive from the R&D process beavering away on new technological potentials and seeking to find applications for these potentials, while the latter proposes that innovations are stimulated by a search for ways to solve social problems or meet what are perceived to be unfulfilled demands. In practice both processes are at work, although at particular periods, and in particular areas of development, one may dominate over the other.

A particularly interesting formulation of the issues involved has recently been made by Metcalfe (1986), who points out that in practice the environment of innovation involves a complex interplay between technology-push and demand-pull, in which a selection process of a sort is operating. Rather than there being one innovation which fulfils one function, the situation more often is that several alternative technologies are in existence, whose design characteristics overlap so that they each perform more or less well across a range of functions. (Thus, VTRs and videodiscs both display recorded movies, but the former allow for home recording, while the latter provide better-quality images; in the case of many long-established household activities such as transport, lighting, heating, etc., there are many quite distinct types of product which aim to satisfy consumer needs.) Metcalfe points out that each of the alternative technologies is a potential site for R&D which can improve design characteristics, lower costs, etc., and argues that feedback from market reactions to alternative offerings is an important determinant of which systems get developed further. He points out, in the course of his study, that this may well mean that a technically inferior product becomes the innovation and diffusion leader, simply because of its market leverage at a particular time or place. We might note that this point can be generalised: it may be that often the technological choices that lead to particular HI products first becoming available are the result of decisions as to profitable lines of IT R&D based on perceptions of industrial rather than consumer markets. For much consumer technology is the result of technology transfer from the formal economy, and, as we argued in Chapter 1, HI has tended—for reasons of scepticism and snobbery—to be regarded as peripheral to the important areas of advanced IT.

3.5 Diffusion and technology transfer

There is nothing new in the perception that consumer products, especially those used in the informal economy for household members to produce their own goods and services, can very often be viewed as 'technology transfers' from production processes in the formal economy to those in the domestic informal economy. Basic innovations in heartland technologies like cheap motor power, petrochemicals, electronics, and now microelectronics, are often applied to processes in the home in much the same way that they had earlier been applied to industrial production processes.

Typically, new products are at first too expensive for application to these household activities; they are employed on a large scale by industry only, until continued innovation and economies of scale allow substantial reduction in costs or adaptation of technologies to household circumstances. Not only the price, but also the size of many industrial devices, for example, is quite inappropriate for private homes, and likewise their noise levels, power consumption, or requirements for skills are too great.

There are many examples of this technology transfer process. For instance, washing machines, water heaters, vacuum cleaners, motor cars, telephones, power tools, and many more, follow upon innovations in motors and energy control, metal machining and electronics, which were first applied to similar products in industry. It is interesting to note that a kind of hierarchy of diffusion trajectories seems to be implied in many accounts: first manufacturing, then services, and finally consumers. Thus, industrial engineering preceded commercial power laundries, which preceded domestic electrical washing machines. This pattern may not apply so clearly in the case of IT, where leading-edge applications are often being made in advanced branches of services (such as banking).

This process of technology transfer has several important features. First, industry may be a test-bed for the new technologies. As well as pioneering the processes involved to the point that economies of scale in production can be realised, industrial use can support the standardisation of methods, the development of practical knowledge about the technologies, and can originate the network within which diffusion is facilitated (as noted above). Industrial application of the technology can lead to the improvement of its reliability and efficiency in order to reduce consumer fears about its viability and present and future usefulness.

Second, industry, and other branches of the formal economy (e.g. the education system), can also play an important role as demonstrator of new products and processes. It can familiarise consumers with the advantages (and limitations) of the new technologies, by putting them into contact with the devices at the workplace, or as consumers of services which use the devices in their branches. Thus, professional and clerical workers learn what can be expected from microcomputers from their use of them in offices, and industrial workers similarly acquire knowledge of microprocessor-controlled tools. Clients of services are similarly exposed to new technologies when banks and libraries installing viewdata terminals, visiting service workers (meter readers, insurance sales personnel) bring portable computers with them, and restaurants use microwave cookers. (Of course this is nothing new: experience with TV, for example, was rapidly gained when bars introduced TV sets to entertain their clientele.) The educational system may play a particularly important role in familiarising young people with new technologies—thus the significance attributed to the installation of microcomputers in schools.

But, third, technology transfer is a complex process, going beyond simple imitation. New products may be used in quite different ways in different branches of industry. This reflects the distinct specific tasks of particular branches. Take the example of TV systems: these are used for security purposes in banks, for example, but in manufacturing industries the function of cathode ray tubes is more likely to be that of testing the performance of electronic circuits, while in power stations they are used both to display data about the functioning of the complex system, together with the monitoring of events in hostile environments. The picture is even more complicated where transfers of technologies to households are concerned, on account of the specific purposes of household activities, as well as because of the relatively limited resources possessed by consumers.

Firms may differ in their core tasks, but they are all in the business of making profits. Even public services face financial controls and targets, which often lead them to make decisions about work organisation and technical choice that parallel those (indeed, often imitate those) of private firms. Consumers may wish to save their money, and to minimise the informal work that they need to put into domestic tasks. But, in contrast to most institutions in the formal economy, they also seek enjoyable leisure pursuits to occupy the time freed by saving on informal work. Harmonious interpersonal relations, a comfortable environment, even self-realisation of family members, are of more concern for the typical family budgeter than they are for the typical manager (except where they relate to the manager's own work, or have been put on the agenda by organisational development problems or strong and progressive trade unionism).

This means, for example, that successful consumer product innovations may well share the labour-saving and convenience-enhancing features of industrial applications. But there will be many cases in which what are at heart the same technologies are applied for purposes that are at best infrequently encountered in the formal economy. Thus household use of TV screens is dominated by entertainment uses—the consumption of TV broadcasts, and more recently, the playing of video games and recorders, and the leisure use of home computers. Possible future applications of TV in the home, ironically, are more like industrial uses, for example 'peritelevision' (monitoring domestic equipment) and closed-circuit video for home security.

This discussion provides some useful pointers to the speed and direction of

HI innovations. For example, it suggests that some forecasts of rapid development of home automation systems may be a little premature, given that office automation and, in particular, 'smart buildings' (the closest industrial analogues) have yet to take off to any degree. They still face problems associated with lack of standardisation and difficulties in choosing between competing systems and in determining patterns of work organisation. So far the 'smart building' is mainly a prestige development of very affluent firms.

The British experience with Prestel, a viewdata system, would seem to confirm this view of the facilitating effect of business experience on the development of consumer HI. What was initially seen as a new system that would cater to the mass public was found to have most appeal for business applications. But the French experience with the Minitel system indicates that in an appropriate environment such a consumer market can develop, and in many respects set the pace for business users. (This case will be discussed more in Chapter 4, but we can note here that the French consumer was not faced with the decision as to whether to invest in equipment, at least not to the same extent as the British, because basic terminals were provided free of charge: the market decision then is less centred on the technology as hardware, and more on the use of new technology-based services.)

Indeed, our view of the likely applications of IT in the home could even be over-influenced by current industrial experience. There may well be innovations in the household use of the basic technologies, such that the main developments in HI will differ from IT's industrial applications to much the same extent as entertainment TV differs from industrial use of the CRT. Such innovations may be developed by households themselves, as more or less spontaneous changes in ways of life (analogous to the industrial learning process). Most commonly, of course, the key innovations derive from the manufacturers of the new consumer hardware itself, when they are able to identify a mass market or market niche for a substantially new product. Television may seem to be an exemplary case of this, but it should give pause for thought, since the key innovations may be more to do with the 'software' of TV broadcasts than with its hardware and infrastructure.

Associated with the physical innovations of TV and TV broadcasting were substantive innovations on the part of the service industries responsible for programming and programme content. It is significant that early expectations were that TV would essentially be a substitute for physical attendance at scheduled theatre performances, sporting occasions, etc. The TV set itself was seen as a mini-theatre, with curtains and all. But, in practice, a whole range of televisual forms has been invented, such as news analysis and soap operas, situation comedies and natural history documentaries, cartoons and commercials. A range of watching styles has also emerged, with TV often being simply 'moving wallpaper' rather than a little stage in the corner of the room. Similar surprises in the application of new technologies in the home are often associated with service innovations that complement the new hardware. For example, the main home computer application to date has been arcade-style games, rather than the database management and other industrial-type applications anticipated by early commentators. The French viewdata system's great successes are in interpersonal messaging services—the messagerie—rather than in providing access to databases.

Perhaps there are lessons here for forecasts of the development of HI. We should beware of assuming that just because something can be done in the home, or even because it can be demonstrated as already being done extremely effectively in business environments, it will actually find success as a consumer technology. In order to forecast the likely trajectories of HI, we need to bear in mind the specific requirements of households (and how these may be changing), and the strategies adopted by hardware, software and infrastructure suppliers to find ways of meeting these requirements. One feature of IT—its malleability, the applicability of the same technology to many diverse ends—makes it likely that one or other supplier will be successful in this in most areas of everyday life. But these features also make it possible for policymaking bodies to intervene in the course of HI development—although these interventions inevitably take place against a backdrop of private sector innovations that follow national and transnational market dynamics which local and national agencies may have little ability to influence.

3.6 Forecasting the future—and creating it

The previous sections of this chapter provide a number of reasons why the art of predicting consumer demand for substantially new goods and services is liable to be very subject to error, why forecasts have to be seen in terms of the assumptions that the forecasters are bringing to bear towards the topic. There are no behavioural data—for example trends in expenditure of the products—that can be extrapolated. And, unlike the situation for slight modifications of established products, when a really novel product has yet to become available in the marketplace, it is exceedingly difficult to use conventional market research tools such as those based on attitude measures.

Standard approaches to assessing consumer preferences, for example by asking for opinions about the desirability of a product ('how much would you be prepared to pay for this?') or about which of several options would be chosen if one was in the market for a new gizmo ('which of these looks like the best buy to you?'), are invalidated by the absence of concrete experience on which perceptions can be based. At best one will be eliciting responses concerning behaviour in a situation that is at present purely hypothetical—and that is one in which many of the parameters identified above as of major import will be vaguely specified. Reactions to a product may very much depend upon expectations concerning price, user-friendliness, obsolescence, and even diffusion rates themselves—the latter being the very thing most suppliers will be interested in predicting (although good marketing practice would lead them to pay attention to the salience of the other issues in consumer judgements!).

As the heart of a technological revolution which means that really novel products are emerging alongside improvements of familiar products, IT is giving rise to growing problems for forecasters. One consequence of this is an increased potential for self-fulfilling and self-negating prophecies in the field of HI. Self-fulfilling prophecies are forecasts whose influence is such that they help to bring about the state of affairs which they purportedly report on in an objective manner. In the case of consumer goods, for example, the dissemination of forecasts suggesting that a particular standard may come to dominate may well help to bring this situation about. In contrast, self-negating prophecies undermine a state of affairs that might otherwise have developed, for example by convincing people that this is a future to be avoided. Thus, predictions that a new medium or mode of delivery (e.g. DBS) will lead to a deterioration in content standards may lead to pre-emptive legislation to restrict the diffusion of the medium, or to regulations governing content (e.g. controls on violent programmes, target levels of locally-produced content).

In several countries, especially in Western Europe, expectations of major consumer markets for HI have been tempered by the (real or apparent) failure of some of the devices and services currently on offer. We have already touched on two examples of this. The first is viewdata, where, with the exception of France, services have to date failed to achieve anything like the consumer markets originally anticipated for them; and their modest perform-ance has been visibly contrasted to the fanfare of publicity attending their launch. The second is home computers, which in the early 1980s had become a thriving industry in the United Kingdom, and were seen by many as the proof of the arrival of 'information society'. The booming home computer market suffered a slump in sales in the mid-1980s; and what in retrospect looks like a classic industry shake-out such as is often experienced early in the product cycle, with a large proportion of the new firms manufacturing specific models of home computer going out of business, was widely seen as the end of an illusion, the bursting of a bubble. Investors reacted by moving from an extreme of euphoria with IT shares to considerable caution—though admittedly this also reflected similar difficulties in the business micro-computer sector.

Nevertheless, certain areas of consumer electronics have developed re-markably buoyant markets, and would appear to be well past take-off on a logistic curve. In recent years the extent of market growth has been such that both VTRs and CD players have evoked fears on the part of Europeans, since these are in large part Japanese imports. Digital audio tape recorders (DAT) are now attracting attention both as a threat to existing audio products (including the developing European CD industry!), and as being liable to dramatically increase piracy of the 'software' of recorded music. And trade in entertainment services, notably those associated with developments in satellite and Cable TV, have led to cultural as well as economic worries (in Canada as well as Europe). Doubts have been raised concerning the future of Europe's remaining capacity to produce consumer electronic devices and the (largely entertainment) software they use.

These concerns have been reflected in the activity of government agencies and industrial groups. But these activities have largely been carried out as matters of short-term industrial policy ('give our electronics firms some breathing space') or cultural policy ('keep our media under national control'). They have been at some considerable remove from the specific themes of government IT policy. The focus of such IT policy *per se* (e.g. Britain's Alvey programme, the European Community's Esprit and RACE programmes) has largely remained upon R&D in frontier technologies and to a lesser extent on industrialf applications, as we noted in Chapter 1. These policies have substantial long-term implications for HI, but this is usually incidental to their purposes—a consumer spin-off, as it were, from scientific and industrial developments. HI itself has rarely cropped up as an important area for activity in the various 'Fifth Generation' programmes that are under way—although it is worth noting that there are many Japanese statements to the effect that pursuing improvements in Human-Machine Interfaces is a pre-requisite for the diffusion of advanced IT to final consumers.

This is not to deny that many agencies have launched programmes that seek to apply IT to social objectives, or more often to provide a 'technology assessment' of the implications of new technologies. But these tend to be uncoordinated and to have little direct linkage to more general industrial policies. (An example of such a linkage would be the policy of buying locally-manufactured equipment when computerisation of parts of the health service is being undertaken.) The more ambitious efforts to achieve coordination of IT-based social and welfare innovations to date have mostly remained only at the stage of preliminary studies and experiments. Furthermore, they have typically been initiatives of local and regional government, as if in response to local concerns about the long-term consequences of national priorities for grass-roots objectives. And since they have often stemmed from 'Green' or left-wing political groups (responding to more conservative national govern-ments), their foci have tended to be on environmental and workplace issues.

The efforts of the Greater London Council (GLC), up to its abolition in 1986, in daring to promote economic strategies based on an entirely different set of premises from those of the Thatcher government, are a case in point. The GLC set out to develop plans, and planning systems, for cable and new technologies in the London area, setting these in the context of more general industrial and employment strategies. But, with the exception of the 'New Technology Networks' and some projects supported by the Greater London Enterprise Board, on the one hand, and some schemes to promote 'commun-ity computing' and the training of disadvantaged groups in IT skills on the other, its ambitious IT initiatives remained largely a pencil-and-paper activity. (Though it should be acknowledged that part of its purpose was to provide a model for national government policy should the Labour opposition come to power).[5]

Another interesting example is the Sotech Programme of the State Government of Nordrhine-Westphalia, as described in the newsletter *Sotech Rundbrief*.[6] This sponsors action research (including awareness activities) in both employment/workplace issues and in welfare and education services and 'home and everyday life'. In the latter area, the projects supported to date are largely social scientific research into possible consequences of the introduction of IT (EFT, new media, home computers), and awareness activities (women and new technologies, how to shape technological development), together with some action research (access to media for the elderly, application of IT to disabled people). Several projects aimed at using the Minitel/Teletel system for local social objectives are now under way in France.

Thus, although initiatives consciously bearing on HI have been undertaken, they are few, and tend to be experimental projects. The importance of their demonstration and awareness activities should not be underestimated; and we shall see that they may be significant in developing 'trigger markets' for HI. The best of these projects may be seen as efforts to effect a 'technology transfer' of IT to marginalised sections of the community and to social movements; as both attempting a wider diffusion of IT potentials than the market alone might achieve, and to enable social groups to play a more active role in shaping technologies to their own requirements.

But at present it seems fair to conclude that by far the greater influence on HI is the dynamic of policies undertaken with respect to telecommunications and electronics industries—and, of course, the strategies of these industrial actors themselves. For various reasons, the pressure on governments to take action in respect of these industries is high. Decisionmakers are being confronted with choices with an urgency that poses considerable problems for 'technology assessment' of possible social consequences, or of the shaping of programmes to achieve social goals. These important issues may often be written off as pointless luxuries by a government official confronted with a balance of payments crisis or the threatened closure of a major plant in a region of high unemployment. Thus, the shaping of the future may well be a by-product of more immediate concerns: and forecasts that depict a view of the future without indicating how to intervene in affairs are merely part of a larger tendency.

And, indeed, this book will have to plead guilty to displaying this tendency. The decisions being taken are so numerous, the areas that are interrelated so diverse, and the issues raised so complex, that more than a touch of humility is called for. It seems more urgent to seek to shed light on the developing state of affairs, and in particular to identify some of the main forces that underlie current and future developments, than to write a premature manifesto for action. We shall, however, be able to identify some points at which leverage might be obtained, and will conclude this book with some ideas about how to go about determining what is to be done.[7]

Meanwhile, the following chapters seek to set out the approaches being pursued by some of the major actors in HI and fields bearing on it. ('Some of' because we shall not, notably, be treating the role of the financial and retail organisations that are of critical importance in establishing Electronic Funds Transfer, 'smart' cards, and teleservices, nor the automobile manufacturers who are supplying consumer IT as in-car systems.) Chapter 4 addresses the area of telecommunications policy, where considerable change and variety has been apparent in government strategies, and where direct consequences for final consumer services are significant. HI services like viewdata have developed within the context of these telecommunications strategies. We then turn to policies with respect to specific items of consumer electronics, in Chapter 5. Finally, in Chapter 6, we consider what these developments may mean for the 'home of the future', considering both specific areas of household activity and the approaches that are being developed in the 'smart house/home automation' field.

Notes

1. I have here drawn on data and insights presented by Leslie Haddon of Imperial College, London, in draft chapters for his PhD dissertation (i.e. Haddon, 1987). This author has also related current debates about HI to discussions of the 'home of the future' in earlier decades.
2. For a survey of the industrial innovation literature, see Freeman (1982); for a more 'economics-oriented' approach, see Coombs et al. (1987). Good surveys of the diffusion literature are provided by Rogers (1983, 1986), in the latter case with reference to communications technologies. For an interesting application of theoretical (curve-fitting) models to a range of consumer behaviours, see Hamblin et al. (1974); as far as I know the original approach developed by these authors has not been further explored in any depth. Another line of analysis, which has not yet been developed in sufficient detail to deal with many HI products, is the analysis of elasticities of demand: see Bosworth (1987) for a comparative review of data conducted with thoughts of IT in mind.
3. See, in particular, Hartley et al. (1985); Williams and Mills (1986) present an interesting collection of studies of attitudes to technological change, prepared as part of the same programme. There is relatively little discussion of the role of consumer choices in the construction of new technologies: but see the collections edited by Bijker et al. (1987), and MacKenzie and Wajcman (1985), and references in Haddon (1987).
4. User-supplier networks are discussed by Guile (1986) with respect to manufac- turing IT; see also the work of Freeman (1982) and papers in Macleod (1986).
5. See GLC (1986), GLEB (1986), Wield (1987).
6. Schatz-Bergfeld (1986); the Sotech Rundbrief is issued by the Minister für Arbeit, Gesundheit und Soziales des Landes Nordrhein-Westfalen. The IRIS project of the European Community should also be mentioned; this established an inventory of IT innovations applied to social objectives, although the expected next step—a major programme of research on this topic—has not (so far?)

materialised. (See, for example, Gleave (1986), which includes a large number of welfare innovations as well as many that could be classified as HI—viewdata and teletext services, and emergency alarms, for example.) An extensive review of efforts to apply IT innovatively to 'problems of everyday life' in Europe is provided by Cappechi, Pesce and Schiray (1986): this describes some of the Minitel/Teletel experiments mentioned in the text.

7. For essays discussing some of these broader issues and the actors involved in IT development see Finnegan *et al.* (1987).

4 Telecommunications: only connections?

4.1 Telecommunications policy and new consumer services

Telecommunications policy has been in a state of considerable flux since at least the mid-1970s. Economic, political and technological forces have prompted remarkable change in both the institutional structure and the long-term visions of communications organisations—both conventional telecommunication and mass media. Telecommunications have come to be seen as the 'information society' equivalent of the railways of early industrial society, as the web that binds together otherwise isolated components of IT. Indeed, the term 'Information Technology' describes the convergence of computers and telecommunications—which has had substantial impacts on both computer and communications industries. For example, computer-to-computer communications have grown explosively, leading to new demands on telecommunications providers (e.g. quality of transmission facilities) and computer suppliers (e.g. interconnection standards); and new transmission and switching systems have been enabled by innovations in microelectronics, optronics and space technology.

Our brief overview of these issues will involve first, a discussion of the current processes of deregulation and regulation of telecommunications, and second, a discussion of the technological changes associated with the digitalisation of the telecommunications infrastructure. We shall then consider new services that are based on telecommunications, and finally set out a view of the future of computer-communications systems.

4.2 Changing regulatory regimes in telecommunications

The evolution of telecommunications itself has involved rapid, and sometimes contradictory, developments in two sectors, exemplifying the 'convergence' associated with IT developments. These two sectors, telecommunications and mass media industries, have both been subject to pressures to change their regulatory structures throughout the West.

The traditional structure of the telecommunications system in OECD countries involved a number of typical features.[1] In most countries, the telecommunications infrastructure was provided as a public utility and basic national resource by the combined post and telecommunications authority (PTT); the private North American telephone companies functioned in a regulatory environment that produced many similarities in practice to the

PTT structure. The PTT would normally be a major employer, and its workforce was typically skilled and highly unionised. It had close relations with the national manufacturers of such electronic equipment as switching apparatus and telephones; in some instances it actually owned these, in most cases it provided them with R&D and other support, and a practically guaranteed market. Likewise there were close relations and in many respects a shared culture with relevant branches of the civil service: this culture included, for example, a common public service ethos (e.g. emphasising universal service provision over strictly commercial principles), and common views of the role of natural monopolies (e.g. acceptance of the value of avoiding the needless duplication of facilities, and thus an emphasis on non-market ways of protecting consumer interests in the absence of competition).

A powerful set of interests was brought into being by these arrangements. And, like many other complex sets of social interests, over time pressures for change confronted forces that sought stability in the regulatory structure. The strength of these factors, and of the groups involved, has led to a divergent pattern of evolution of telecommunications regimes across Western countries.

Let us briefly outline some of these cross-cutting interests. *Consumer groups* are, of course, at the core of our interest in HI, but they are not typically particularly influential in telecommunications policy. They would typically be concerned about maintaining universal access to telecommunications facilities, so that, for example, rural areas would not lack services (or be forced to pay considerably more for services) that could be provided most economically for urban agglomerations. However, in some countries, such as Britain, private consumers were by no means happy with existing PTT services—for example, with the price and quality of telephony, with the time taken to install connections and the variety of equipment available.

Business Users have experienced changing telecommunications needs. As some sectors have become dependent upon computer operations, so data communications linking systems at different sites became more important—and, with them, requirements for reliable and high-volume communications networks. This has led many large firms to invest in their own private networks, to challenge PTT provisions and pricing, and to complain about divergence in national regimes and problems with transnational communications. Smaller firms rarely share these concerns, and are often more interested in cheap universal provision of basic services: in some countries—such as West Germany—small firms have had considerable influence on policymaking.

PTT employees have been concerned that a change in the ethos of the telecommunications system towards more competition would lead to threats to their job security. Such concerns are being expressed by Australian unions at the time of writing. The fear is that there will be greater emphasis on savings of labour costs, an erosion of civil-service-type conditions of employment, and a shift to part-time work; to this is added the concern of technical workers that R&D may be cut back. However, management and some other technical workers may welcome liberalisation: they see opportunities for more career advancement, and perhaps greater freedom to achieve wage levels similar to those in comparable private firms.

Established equipment suppliers were aware of threats to their established markets, of course, although in some instances they saw opportunities to gain overseas markets in a general climate of liberalisation. But the convergence of computing and telecommunications was also bringing *new equipment suppliers* onto the scene. In some cases with more facility at providing advanced IT systems. These wanted to demonstrate their capability in the provision of telecommunications systems and devices: and, for example, suppliers of computer-communications systems, Local Area Networks (LANs) and new private exchanges sought to exercise more influence over the regulatory environment. It is widely believed within the supply industries that general liberalisation of markets will prove many national suppliers unviable: it is argued that most national markets are too small to support the large volumes of R&D and investment necessary for new systems. This is leading many observers in Europe to call for the establishment of a European telecommunications market and the rationalisation of the supply industries so as to achieve economies of scale and global competitiveness. But it is also suggested that some European suppliers, not used to competition or even to ploughing back sufficient profits into R&D, have at best a limited chance of surviving in the absence of national 'shelters'.

Civil servants confronted pressures from all these groups (and their overt and covert political representatives). They were confronted with growing pressure to establish new regulatory regimes; and while these offered prospects for new career paths, they would also require considerable changes in their own knowledge base and organisational culture. An example of this is Britain's having set up a new Office of Telecommunications (Oftel) to 'police' the liberalised telecommunications regime: this has provided new opportunities for promotion, but in common with regulatory agencies everywhere there are problems for the civil service in gaining expertise that can verify claims, from the regulated industries, concerning where the boundaries can be drawn between purely technical and more commercial/political issues!

The process of change in regulatory regimes worldwide has been very much influenced by the rapid pace that it has taken on in the United States. Following protracted legal action, AT&T submitted to divestiture in 1984, establishing a series of regional operating companies. This splitting-up of AT&T's regional operations was followed by the granting of permission for AT&T to enter computer, office automation and information services markets. The consequences of these developments are not easy to summarise. It is generally argued that the rapid growth of new telecommunications services has been facilitated; and, despite consumer complaints about the quality and pricing of service, long-distance and high-volume charges have been reduced, benefiting business users. (Alternative telecommunications networks had been in existence before divestiture, with business networks having been able to resell their facilities for some time, but competition for long-distance traffic has subsequently been intense.)

As the American market became more open to competition from Western Europe and Japan, so US firms added their pressure to calls for change in regulatory structures in these regions. The United Kingdom privatised British Telecom in late 1984, and allowed Mercury Communications to compete in the provision of a national network. (This has to date been largely involved in providing business telecommunications, but private consumer telephone services are beginning to become available from Mercury, although their take-up remains very limited.) Again, long-distance calls have been cheapened relative to local call rates. Japan has similarly privatised NTT, the local PTT, and allowed for competition in the supply of telecommunications facilities (although there is persistent and loud criticism from foreign equipment suppliers about the degree to which liberalisation has been effective). Less dramatic steps towards 'deregulation' in effect, a new regulatory regime featuring increased liberalisation) have been taken by several other Western countries (e.g. Canada and the smaller European economies).

In contrast, the French and West German (and Australian) PTTs have confronted pressures for change with quite different stances. The French PTT is seen as an important actor in industrial policy, and one that can be spurred towards greater innovation in support of a programme of national modernisation. In common with the Deutsche Bundespost, emphasis is put on engineering standards for a reliable network, and the maintenance of universal service provision. Both countries have recently begun to open up their market for equipment supply, and France is reportedly liberalising its market for Value-Added Network Services.

While the situation for the PTTs remains fluid, convergence also brings mass media into the telecommunications policy arena. The public telephone system (PSTN) is able to carry entertainment services, for example some viewdata services, while future improvements in telecommunications infrastructure—going beyond the ISDN plans to provide channel capacities more in line with those provided on some specialised business lines, or on CATV systems—may mean that video images can be transmitted alongside voice and data. Thus, in the United States, Southern Bell (one of the products of the AT&T break-up) is reportedly working with housing developers to deliver CATV material through new telephone lines rather than dedicated cables, and plans to provide ISDN to 20 per cent of its private consumers by 1991.[2]

Meanwhile, media that were previously the vehicle for TV transmission (e.g. CATV) are being rendered suitable for telephone and computer communications, and some existing systems are already being promoted as suitable not only for consumer services but also for business applications such as videoconferencing, and public service applications such as medical and educational access to videodisc libraries of, for example, X-ray images and detailed maps. There are prospects for integrating communications systems of very different kinds; the issue arises of how far the 'information society' will be brought into being through the PSTN or other networks.

In the United Kingdom, for example, government policy in the early 1980s proposed that the 'cabling of Britain' was something that would most naturally and effortlessly take place by means of allowing new cable TV systems to be established—in other words, entertainment, the demand for new TV channels, would be the 'trigger service' for new telecommunications capacity.[3] A regulatory authority (the Cable Authority, which works together with Oftel) was established to grant licences to consortia which allowed them to establish a cable monopoly in various parts of the country; the criteria that the Cable Authority uses are intended to promote the establishment of higher technology cable systems such as can support new interactive services. Following a major growth in US cable TV in the 1970s, other European countries looked afresh at cable: expansion of networks is generally planned, and the upgrading of systems in those countries where there is already high penetration (e.g. Belgium, Denmark and the Netherlands). However, there are various ways in which this is being carried out—some countries are based on PTT cable provision—and various efforts to regulate material carried by the networks. In addition to the interests affected by the regulatory regime with respect to the PSTN, cable is naturally of significant concern to national broadcasting authorities, who fear an erosion of their audiences if new entertainment services proliferate, and who also raise the threat to national language and to cultural industries supported by broadcasting.

Direct Broadcast Satellite (DBS) is often portrayed as a direct competitor to cable as a means of disseminating TV programmes, although in practice existing cable systems are very often relaying broadcasts from satellites (as we saw in the Captain Midnight case). High-power DBS has been available in Japan since 1986. In Western Europe and North America satellite channels have been available since 1983 and 1984 respectively, but issues such as advertising (national standards vary), language and other differences (hindering European cooperation in programming), and uncertainties concerning costs, have caused problems. However, in 1988 the medium-power Astra satellite is to be launched, relaying sixteen channels (up to eleven of them English-language, with opportunities to choose one's national language to accompany many broadcasts), and there are plans to sell cheap (about £300) dishes and decoders on a large scale (sales of half a million in the first year are forecast by one British retailer). High-power DBS is planned for Europe in the late '90s.

One recent development that is already entangled in the DBS/cable issue is the international debate around new types of TV system (widescreen TV, and high-definition TV—HDTV, which offers considerably improved quality pictures). European actors have opposed Japanese–American proposals for standards for these new types of TV, with technical and commercial concerns intermingling much as they did around earlier TV standards. DBS and cable are liable to be boosted when these new forms of TV become available, since they offer channel capacity required for quality broadcasts. We shall discuss HDTV disputes in more detail later; in the DBS context we should note that European suppliers such as Philips are strongly promoting the MAC standard as a framework for future TV transmissions. MAC's virtues are portrayed as being that it is compatible with both US and Japanese 60 Hz, and European 50 Hz transmission systems; it is optimised for DBS (thus smaller dishes can be used), and it allows for gradual upgrade of TV transmitters and receivers, rather than requiring broadcasters and consumers to start again from scratch (as the competing Japanese system, MUSE, would).[4]

4.3 Towards digital telecommunications systems

The convergence of different telecommunications media, making possible the parallel transmission of voice, data, and video communications over the same network, is facilitated by the fact that these different types of information can be encoded in digital form. They can thus be processed by microelectronic and optronic technology. This has led to a model being developed for a system that can supersede the current PSTN; this is known as the Integrated Services Digital Network (ISDN), as already noted in Chapter 2.

Table 2.3 outlined the improved services that ISDN promises. While its details are still the topic of international deliberation (a complex set of protocols for different types and layers of communication are being established), steps towards digitalisation are being undertaken by most PTTs and telephone companies. There are, however, significant differences in the rate at which progress is being made; for example, the United Kingdom is focusing on providing a service suitable for business users, while West Germany hopes to offer cable connections to all domestic users by the mid-1990s. The United States faces problems owing to the fragmentation of telephone services between different companies: some observers suggest that this will delay the development of a full ISDN; while Japan has announced plans for stepping beyond ISDN to a broadband integrated Network System capable of conveying TV images as well as voice and data traffic.

4.4 Telephony

Telephones have in many ways come to resemble other data-processing devices in the last decade. Table 4.1 outlines some of the features acquired by telephones in recent years. Such features are bound to be augmented in future innovations. We might expect to see them further diffuse, and in addition more technology transfer from the office, for example:

— voice messaging systems;

— phones that are able to re-route calls (so that, for example, the owner can key in a number at which she/he may be contacted, and the call will be automatically transferred, or the phone will notify callers where the owner may be contacted);

— phones that are able to respond only to some classes of caller (based on coded inputs or recognition of the origin number);

— multiple phones in each home, either through small domestic exchanges or innovations that enable a single domestic line to simultaneously carry several voice and data lines;

— and phones linked to 'smart house' equipment and home computers (discussed later).

Table 4.1 Features acquired by household telephones

— Push-button keypads in place of dials.
— Memory features, including automatic redial and the ability to preprogramme commonly-used numbers (state-of-the-art machines can call up such numbers on voice instructions).
— Visual displays in the case of some phones for hearing-disabled people (for example, VDU and electronic typewriter inputs/displays), and phones that can display the number dialled or that is calling in.
— Improved outputs of sound through loudspeakers (again especially useful for handicapped people), and adjustable ringing tones and/or lamp signals.
— Portability, with the cordless phone and cellular phone becoming commonplace.
— Auto-answer facilities, with the attachment of phones to answering machines (with remotely activated playback facilities often now a standard feature).
— Linkage to new services (e.g. Chatline-type 'Talkabout' systems, allowing users to join ongoing conversations.)

These 'smart' features make the telephone more versatile and easy to use, and considerable effort is under way to create more portable phones. While people may not want to be permanently available to callers, one of the major frustrations of contemporary travel (and of the use of many service organisations) is being put out of contact while using the service or being *en route*. Typical situations include being unable to warn people that one's train or plane is delayed, or while experiencing such a delay being unable to consult local timetables to establish whether one will be able to make connections or attend later performances. Thus we would expect diffusion of devices that have many of the features listed in Table 4.1, or else that build on these. For example, future telephones are likely to:

— handle both conventional telephony and data communications;
— have compact and convenient keyboards, with some ability to autodial

familiar names (perhaps searching through a set of numbers if the first does not respond) and to redial numbers;
— have at least a small visual display (to indicate the number being connected to, to display computer, calculator and memory functions such as diary and memo data, and to display written text such as notes or teletext).
— have many of the features of 'smart' home phones, such as being able to hold incoming calls;
— and to be able to operate over long distances (using cellular systems?) so that one number should suffice to locate any given person (and thus that number may become an integral part of their identity!).

4.5 New consumer telecommunication services 1: viewdata

Improvement in telecommunications infrastructure, and the new mood of market orientation in PTTs, have made possible the innovation of numerous services on the PSTN. Many of these are directed towards business users (e.g. cellular radio, messaging services), although they may eventually find consumer markets (stories that cheap cellular phones were about to appear have been persistent, despite their non-materialisation to date). Many services oriented towards consumers (e.g. recorded information services, 'chatlines' where telephone users can join together for ongoing discussions) are fairly trivial innovations, although some of these have been highly successful in commercial terms. But viewdata (also known as videotex) is rather more significant, and has accordingly attracted considerable attention.[5]

Viewdata was invented at the Martlesham R&D laboratories of the British Post Office in 1972. (British Telecom was later to be split off from the postal services, and it retained this laboratory.) Early publicity about the invention led to interest in several other countries: Canada, France and Japan carried out R&D, which resulted in the development of variants of the same basic idea, operating under different technical standards. At the outset, viewdata was seen as a means of generating more telephone traffic and revenue, especially from private consumers at off-peak periods. Essentially, it uses the PSTN as a low-bandwidth communications link to display information on VDUs; the operating assumption in Britain was that the mass public would gain information from databanks in a form suitable for display on domestic TV sets. Thus the early advertisements for Prestel, as the British viewdata service was called, promised 'A World of Information at your Fingertips'.

Prestel was launched in late 1979—the same year as the administration that subsequently privatised British Telecom was voted into power. In retrospect, although Prestel was seen as one of the more market-oriented branches of British Telecom, the new service is seen as having been driven more by the enthusiasm of technical experts (and a public service ethos that emphasised the provision of library-type facilities online to subscribers), than by an adequate analysis of public demand for data services.

Uptake of the product was soon recognised to be falling far short of expectations. Many potential information providers were deterred by the difficulties of rendering their information in a useful form of BT computers. (They were unable to use 'gateways' to their own computers for some years, and this made the implementation of real-time services like teleshopping, as opposed to information-access only, extremely difficult.) And some information providers provided rather low-quality, experimental services, with poor menus and large sections that were incomplete. Prestel thus began as a 'common carrier' service, leaving information providers to supply data—but information providers were very unevenly prepared to launch their services, their databases were of very disparate quality and often poorly indexed.

The general public lacked enthusiasm for a service that:

— required a subscription charge and whose pricing furthermore appeared obscure;
— required a telephone socket installation (at this time quite unusual; subsequently, with a move to multi-telephone households, this has become fairly common);
— required a new television receiver or a relatively expensive adaptor (early models cost around £200) to be added to an existing set;
— was operated by a small and relatively primitive keypad, which was suitable for only the most basic responses;
— did not convincingly appear to offer services that were not already available through existing information outlets, and those that it did offer were not readily distinguishable from those also being offered through the parallel (and often confusable) innovation of teletext.

Additional criticisms were levelled at the early Prestel system: of course, it should be pointed out that, as a world leader, it was bound to have its share of learning difficulties. But the upshot was that Prestel found itself being predominantly used as a business service, particularly as the tour operators found viewdata an appropriate medium for disseminating information about flights and holidays, and their availability, to travel agents—and one whose interactivity (especially when gateways became available) made possible online booking services. (This fuelled a healthy market in specialised viewdata terminals, and private viewdata services—effectively competing with Prestel and getting around some of the shortcomings with which it confronted specialised users—were set up in travel, finance and other sectors.) After two years operation, in early 1982 the common carrier philosophy was modified,and emphasis shifted to 'trigger services', forms of information—and more importantly, interactivity—that would appeal to certain classes of consumer. In other words, the strategy became one of marketing services rather than selling a technology or promoting Prestel as a whole. Instead of referring to 'information providers', 'service providers' were identified. (This was perhaps more a change in emphasis than a qualitative break: from its early days, efforts had been made to establish uses for Prestel appropriate to disabled people and community groups.)

Several significant trigger services, for example home banking, were established in Prestel's shift of direction in the early 1980s. But the sharpest increase in consumer use of Prestel was brought about by the diffusion of home computers, which could be adapted as convenient viewdata terminals by the use of a modem, and appropriate software. An IT-literate market was established, with a shared interest in services surrounding home computers— news and product reviews, telesoftware delivery, messaging, chatlines and enquiries, and computer-related teleshopping.

Private consumers still constitute somewhat under half of the 70,000 Prestel users, but since 1982 this has been a rapidly growing sector. In particular, many home computer owners found that relevant services on Prestel were appropriate to their interests—in exchanging software and graphics, in keeping up with news on IT developments, in corresponding with other computer users. Prestel Microcomputing, with areas like the 'Art Gallery', and the 'Midnight Micronetter's Club', has been one of the most popular areas of the system, with users accessing it through their home computers (and suitable modems)—which allow for much more convenient and versatile use than the original Prestel terminals. Viewdata services have thus helped establish a small base of users able to experiment with other forms of computer-communications: and bulletin boards and small-scale viewdata services have become popular among computer hobbyists. An interesting recent development is that British Telecom has itself been competing with its own Prestel service: it has been targeting microcomputer users for its Telecom Gold service, which although primarily an electronic mail system set up for business users, also offers access to databases and other interactive services; and has also made available MUD, one of a number of online multi-player games for computer users (other such games, with names like 'Shades' and 'Gods', are accessible through Prestel or by directly dialling a host computer).

Several other countries have followed the Prestel route, with PTTs being disappointed to find that public demand has not materialised on anything like the scale anticipated for viewdata services, and subsequently reorienting these services to business users and 'trigger groups'. Table 4.2 reports on the diffusion of viewdata terminals in Western Europe. (Thirteen countries have adopted the Prestel standard for viewdata.) In the United States, several efforts to establish consumer viewdata services (by publishing and other media interests in particular) have foundered, as has Canada's ambitious Telidon experiment. But France, with its Minitel/Teletel service, represents a case apart. (Table 4.3 compares diffusion patterns in Britain, France and West Germany.)

Research on this system began shortly after the first invention of viewdata,

Table 4.2   Viewdata terminals in use in Western Europe, 1985

Country	Terminals (thousands)	Percentage share
Austria	8	0.6
Belgium	2	0.2
Denmark	4	0.3
Finland	4	0.3
France	1000	78.3
Fed. Rep. Germany	70	5.5
Ireland	1	0.1
Italy	6	0.5
Netherlands	25	2.0
Norway	>1	0.5
Spain	3	0.2
Sweden	25	2.0
Switzerland	>3	0.3
United Kingdom	125	9.8

Note: These data refer to viewdata terminals in operation, but do not distinguish between consumer and business users, nor between users of public and private viewdata services.

Source: Butler Cox & Partners Ltd.

Table 4.3   Diffusion patterns of viewdata in three countries
(thousands of subscribers)

	1982	1983	1984	1985	1986	1987
Britain	19.8	38.0	48.0	59.0	70.0	76.0
France	—	120.0	530.0	1,300	2,200	3,000
Germany	—	10.2	21.3	38.9	58.4	83.6

Source: Mayntz and Schneider (1987); French data for mid-1987 from discussion with French experts.

and there were large-scale trials from 1980 on, but it only became publicly available in 1982. The strategy of the PTT (or, more precisely, the Direction Générale de Télécommunications) was not only to increase public telephone use, but also to promote the electronics and telecommunications supply equipment industries. Thus, two significant steps were taken. The first was to provide a service for which there would be a perceived need: the telephone directory was converted into an online service, replacing printed directories and the enquiry service from telephone operators.

The second step was to provide free Minitel terminals (not TV adaptors) to domestic users: by late 1986 over two million terminals had been distributed. In addition, some 200,000 terminals had also been bought or rented, in some instances in order to make use of superior capabilities such as larger memories; this suggests that the chicken-and-egg problem (without services no users, without users no services) had been overcome. Around five thousand distinct services were available on Teletel by mid-1987, with several tens of millions of calls being made per month.

Thus there has been a substantial growth of traffic and services on the Teletel system, such that the PTT claims to expect to cover the costs of terminals within three years. Developments have not been completely unproblematic, however. One unanticipated consequence was the temporary collapse of the French Packet Switching system owing to overuse, causing businesses dependent on it some considerable trouble! There has also been considerable criticism of the nature of some of Teletel's most successful services, in particular the *'messagerie'* which facilitate interpersonal contacts (and have been used extensively for romantic and not-so-romantic assignations), and other services which are seen as more or less supplying electronic soft porn. On the other hand, it is apparent that viewdata is supplying much-needed access possibilities for otherwise marginalised groups: hearing-disabled people are making extensive use of Teletel (having been largely excluded from the telephone), which makes it possible for them to interact more intensively as a community. (Apparently, means have been spontaneously devised to emulate the types of communication characteristic of sign language in the text format of Teletel.)[6]

Teletel is used by many firms and professionals, but is clearly dominated by consumer use: as with Prestel, however, the key factor seems to be interactivity rather than access to large databases. Interestingly, the importance of interactivity was not initially recognised by the system designers; rather it apparently emerged forcefully as a demand from user groups participating in the early trials (leading to design changes in the Teletel system).

The French PTT saw itself as an *enabler* of new services rather than as itself an *information provider* (with the notable exception of the electronic directory). It was easy for service providers to link their own computers—even quite small ones—to the system, so that a diversity of services was stimulated. Payment for most services is organised through the Kiosque tariff system, introduced in 1984 (simplifying earlier arrangements), in which the PTT is responsible for billing (so that subscription to individual services need not be required, and user's uncertainty about unexpected bills is reduced). Further changes are envisaged in this system, allowing for more flexible pricing. Current activities are also directed towards further distribution of terminals, producing a wider range of terminals (e.g, special Minitel for vision-impaired people, adaptors for microcomputers, terminals suitable for Minitel and Prestel standards).

The differences between Prestel and Teletel partly reflect a process of learning, and the familiar story of the first-comer not achieving the full benefits of a new technology. But they also very much reflect the approaches of the British and French governments and PTTs towards telecommunications policy and its contribution to industrial policy. The British experience has been widely interpreted as casting doubt upon the size of consumer for HI. The French experience has likewise been cited as showing that 'information society' is upon us, and as evidence for the importance of taking new consumer goods and services into full account in developing national IT strategies. We return to the future of such computer communications services shortly; first we discuss a broadcast communication service that has often been confused with viewdata.

4.6 New consumer telecommunication services 2: Teletext

Teletext has often been confused with viewdata, not least in the public mind. It is a form of broadcast information that is also presented in a 'page' format, and for this reason we shall discuss it here rather than along with TV in Chapter 5. The similarities in appearance represent the outcome of a strategy adopted by British viewdata and teletext developers (the Post Office and broadcasting companies) and TV set manufacturers in the 1970s. The decision was taken to present both types of material with common technical standards, making development work easier and promising economies in the manufacture of the microprocessors required to decode and display signals on TV sets. Thus 'World Standard' teletext is similar to Prestel-type viewdata, and the UK format has achieved international diffusion. (Again, the French standard, Antiope, is divergent, and some US teletext services—in general poorly developed—use yet another standard.) British government support for teletext, displayed in the effort put into developing these standards, was motivated by a desire to provide national TV manufacturers with a competitive, leading-edge technology.

Teletext services have developed to uneven degrees in most of Western Europe (see Table 4.4) and in a number of other countries (though not to any great extent in North America). The system appeals to the broadcasting technicians, who are happy to see 'surplus bandwidth' used economically to transmit data in digital form. Teletext services have generally been under the control of broadcasters, and the material transmitted has conformed more to a broadcasting/journalistic mentality than much viewdata material: the aim is not to provide a database so much as a magazine from which viewers can pick and choose.

In different countries, different types of material are most successful: everywhere news and broadcasting schedules are popular, in some countries translation, horseracing or special-interest pages are particularly well-received. Subtitles are important as a means of using the new medium to benefit hard-of-hearing and minority-language TV viewers. A 'trigger service' philosophy seems prevalent among teletext providers, who view their

Table 4.4   The diffusion of teletext receivers in Western Europe

Country	1984	1987 (est)	1990 (est)
Austria	3	11	24
Belgium	4	10	14
Denmark	3	9	15
Finland	3	6	14
France	1	10	25
Fed. Rep. Germany	2	10	25
Netherlands	4	8	15
Norway	3	10	18
Sweden	9	16	30
Switzerland	4	8	12
United Kingdom	8	25	55

Source: Ogilvy & Mather Europe, 1984, *The New Media Review 1984*, London: Ogilvy & Mather, cited by Tydeman and Kelm (1986).

activities as servicing a variety of specific markets that may vary considerably from country to country.

As indicated by the diffusion of teletext TV receivers, the innovation has been a success as a new consumer product: the number of receivers continues to grow in most countries, and technical developments are in hand to increase the number of pages that can be made available and to speed access time to them.

Unlike viewdata, teletext does not require additional expenditure after having acquired the apparatus, and does not involve use of the telephone system. While not truly interactive, it does permit self-directed exploration of a large volume of information, and opportunities exist for responding to advertisements, competitions, etc. via conventional telephony. Teletext has largely been marketed through the standard system of replacement of TV sets (and in the United Kingdom by that country's system of hiring latest-model TV sets). And the services offered have been those deemed relevant by broadcasters.

A recent development has been the use of teletext for busines rather than consumer services: coded material may be distributed cheaply—for example to clients of financial information services or to branches of a retail chain—using teletext, and yield useful royalties to system providers. In some instances, material from these private services may be selectively made available to consumers—for example exchange rates from financial services. The relations between business and consumer services on teletext are developing with different dynamics to those on viewdata, reflecting the features of the two technologies and the different regulatory systems for broadcast versus other data.

As a new telecommunications medium, then, teletext has achieved more widespread penetration and use than viewdata (even, apparently, in France). It has succeeded without the kind of active policy necessary for Teletel's success in France, though it has clearly required the commitment of broadcasting authorities. (Teletext services are often offered as a public service, although advertising is a major source of revenue in some instances.) Government support has nevertheless been important in establishing a framework for teletext development.

In 1987 a rather ironic development was instituted in British and French telecommunications. An agreement was reached whereby BBC's teletext service was made available on Teletel for French viewdata users—another demonstration of the process of convergence at work! It will be interesting to see whether access to material originally developed in a non-interactive medium, but under a magazine-like philosophy, will appeal to users of an interactive medium—especially given that it is in a foreign language. As well as reflecting technological convergence, it is worth noting that this instance is part of a wider strategy to make France the natural hub for new telecommunication services in Europe (and in the world: BBC teletext is available in the United States via Teletel outlets in the US.).

4.7 Consumer applications of computer-communications

Now let us return to computer-communications systems. The services which these offer to domestic consumers can be roughly divided into three groups: information access, transactions, and interpersonal services. As we have already seen, the original expectations for viewdata were that the medium would supply online information services, access to databases. Now the other two functions, which involve high levels of *interactivity*, are accorded rather more prominence: transactional activities and interpersonal communications.

4.7.1. Information access

First, some online information services may well be at a comparative disadvantage to mass data storage systems such as CD-I. Here the different delivery systems may be in competition: some observers claim that the success of CD-ROM in Italy is accounted for by the unreliability of the Italian telephone service (rendering it unhelpful for online data services), while the relative failure of CD-ROM in France relates to the success of Minitel/Teletel, and the consequent focusing of attention on online systems. If one is interested in encyclopaedic knowledge, then mass data storage technologies may be highly appropriate. We consider these technologies in more detail in Chapter 5.

But online services offer some facilities that data storage cannot readily emulate. For example, unless CDs are to be distributed in place of daily newspapers (which is not so inconceivable in terms of new low-cost production techniques which resemble photography), information on topical issues cannot be delivered via this medium. News and sport, weather and traffic information may be handled by conventional broadcast and teletext services. But personal requirements for data on, say, the opening hours of museums and other facilities is harder to deal with by such means, especially for a user who wishes to investigate a range of distinct options. Here higher levels of interactivity become more important.

Apart from information on facilities, consumer analogues of current online professional services may be important. These might include, for example, consumer advice services and reviews of goods and services, if not bibliographic-type data services and access to financial data, which require the immediacy of online communications. Viewdata suppliers are seeking to establish 'trigger markets' among consumer groups with shared interests— owners of particular cars or computers, sports hobbyists, games and music fans, etc. While there is certainly potential for 'magazine'-type services here, it is likely that more interactivity (e.g. question-and-answer sessions, club activities) will often be sought by such groups of consumers.

The attraction of consumer 'magazine' and database services might be considerably extended were considerably improved displays available— whether these be higher-quality VDUs or efficient and cheap printers. Existing 'electronic newspapers' on viewdata (and teletext) services are not very attractive for several reasons:

— the limited amount of text that fits onto a conventional screen;
— the eyestrain often associated with reading it;
— the low portability of the screen (not very comfortable on one's lap, let alone in the bath!);
— and the typically cumbersome menu system which makes it difficult to scan items and use the material in a highly interactive way.

Being able to acquire paper copies quickly, quietly, and without awkward messing around with form feeders would be important. It might well pose a major threat to conventional newspapers; one model that has been suggested is the electronic newspaper supplied via DBS or cable, and printed at home according to consumer specifications (e.g. no sports pages but in-depth financial news). The ultimate display technology must be a 'Smartbook' or successor device of some sort—preferably one that is not rigid but flexible enough to be folded into one's pocket!—with sufficient RAM storage memory that one can download material rather than staying online.

4.7.2. Transactional services

The second class of computer communications services are transactional services, such as teleshopping and telebanking (where money is transferred electronically and, in the former case, items are ordered), and telebooking (the ability to research train and theatre seats remotely). Many experiments with such services have been carried out, but several limitations have become clear with existing viewdata systems in the case of teleshopping, in particular. The shopping process is far more rigid that that undertaken in a physical shop, the amount of information (especially visual information) on products is severely limited—and, of course, delivery remains a problem. On the other hand, recent service developments have attempted to offer consumer choice as to which of a number of time ranges delivery is required in, and the opportunity of setting up and them replicating or modifying a standard shopping list.

Data storage technologies like CD-I would seem to pose little challenge here, since immediacy is of key importance and data inputs from consumers are of the essence. But if one of the major problems of existing teleshopping services is the low quality of the visual and other information offered (compared to conventional visits to shops and browsing through catalogues), and the lack of user-friendliness of viewdata-based shopping systems, then there may be opportunity to apply domestic data storage technologies. Broadband communications, if available, would help cope with the first of these problems (and perhaps with the second too, since sophisticated software and high-level data transfer would be needed if teleshopping were to simulate physical shopping).

In other circumstances, data storage might substitute for data communications, as has already been indicated. Just as department stores and mail order firms publish catalogues of consumer durables, so innovative retailers could move to a CD publishing of catalogues, and link this to computer communications, so that the consumer's system would interrogate the CD for basic product details and video images, with good quality software perhaps emulating a stroll through the shelves and arcades, and then use conventional phone systems to ascertain product availability, current costs and delivery arrangements. This is particularly appropriate to shopping for consumer durables, but is quite conceivable for more frequent shopping arrangements (provided the CDs can be frequently updated as product ranges change).

But large-scale teleshopping is unlikely to emerge speedily without policy interventions. The most successful experiments in the United Kingdom, for example, have been those aimed at housebound and disabled people, and have been organised as much as, or more as, social services as commercial activities. Current industry opinion seems to be that the affluent and busy people who spend enough money to provide a profitable basis for teleshopping are really most interested in using such a service to relieve themselves of routine, low-value shopping, and can somehow find time to shop for high-value items. Physically visiting shops produces social rewards that are absent from teleshopping, in some circumstances at least. On the other hand, there is some evidence that the 'Caditel' system on Minitel is providing a satisfactory basis for everyday grocery shopping, and that the high diffusion of viewdata in France has made it possible for teleshopping to substitute to a significant extent for mail order (over 1 per cent of the turnover of La Redoute, the largest French mail order company).[7]

4.7.3. Interpersonal services

The third class of computer communications services are what we have termed interpersonal (or messaging) services. The popularity of such services has been most clearly demonstrated in France, where Teletel has spawned the *'messagerie'*, which features a high volume of electronic mail and computer-mediated conversation. Indeed, a general conclusion is that public viewdata services seem to be far more attractive as systems for interpersonal communication than as the means of access to massive databases that the authorities originally saw them.[8]

Much of the attraction of these facilities seems to stem from their relative anonymity, so that a variety of erotic fantasising and liaison-formation have been popular types of activity. By late 1986 concerns about possible uses by prostitutes and paedophiles, and reports that alongside romances cases of sexual abuse had occurred, led to PTT efforts to find ways of regulating *messagerie* services. Similar concerns have surfaced in the United Kingdom, with obscene language appearing on some chatlines and bulletin boards. (It has not proved easy, as of yet, to use software to 'filter out' offensive material — high-level expert systems will be needed to cope with racist and sexist innuendo.)

As with many instances of regulating new media in the 1980s — most notably videotapes — the social forces that are concerned about media content are diverse. Often, indeed, they are otherwise antagonistic. For example, homophobes attack 'gay chatlines' on Britain's Prestel; feminists challenge sexually exploitative services on France's Teletel; parents seek to regulate children's communications, and so on. These concerns are bound to apply to newly emerging communications facilities, too: for example, telephone-based chatlines in Britain (which allow several people to talk together, and some of which are specifically targeted at youth) have been 'exposed' as featuring discussions of sex and drugs (and probably rock and roll).

But many other kinds of interpersonal interaction are also significant, not only in public viewdata systems, but also on bulletin boards and other computer communications facilities (such as the US CompuServe network, which has several hundreds of thousands of members, although there is some doubt about how many of these are active users). Many of these are related to professional activities or hobbies, and have close ties with electronic mail and teleshopping. These include:

— 'agony aunts' and various *advice services* (computer topics, of course, and also less serious, jokey services, but also—not always uninterested— advice on topics as various as homework and religious faith, consumer issues and personal problems);
— *chatlines*, where one can add comments to an ongoing conversation which a potentially large number of users may join (some of these are devoted to no specific topic, others are devoted to, for example, political isues, music, sport);
— *computer conferences* where electronic mail messages pursuing a particular topic are distributed to all conference members;
— and combinations of conventional and electronic *mail* (telex, telegram, rapid physical delivery of keyed-in messages, electronic greetings cards, etc.).

Many of these services are used for semi-professional applications or for pursuing hobby interests. Some may be outlets for lonely people. Others are, not surprisingly, largely employed for entertainment purposes. Some inter-personal services—or services that are similar to and often overlap with interpersonal services—are clearly devoted to this purpose. Perhaps most notable here are *telegames*.

Some telegames are no more than conventional computer games—or, at least, those that do not require rapid data-communications and good graphics—in which the user is competing with the computer. But others involve using computer communications as media that *both* structure the game (providing displays of the 'board' or environment, and regulating the system of rules of the game) and mediate the interaction of players. Alongside the application of telecommunications to conventional games like chess, there has been an interesting growth of multi-user role-playing games. These combine the characteristics of computer adventure games, role-playing 'Dungeons and Dragons'-type fantasy games, and *messagerie*. In Britain, MUD (Multi-User Dungeon) was initially developed on a university main-frame computer, but is now available online through a British Telecom computer. (It has been exported to the United States, being available on CompuServe.) In other games, like Shades (on Prestel) and Gods (run by a software company), users take on personae and develop complex relation-ships with each other. On Prestel, games-players can interact with each other outside the game—to arrange meetings, to discuss tactics (and form allian-ces), to announce personal experience and activities in which other players may be interested (e.g. two players getting 'married' within the game).

Computer-communications along the viewdata and CompuServe lines are bound to continue to grow in importance, but in many countries their diffusion will probably continue to be slow and uneven, spreading out from computer hobbyists and professional users. It will certainly depend upon such interlinked factors as:

— the rate of diffusion of domestic equipment that can be linked into computer networks: there are signs that several other countries (notably the Netherlands) are planning to follow the French interventionist strategy for diffusing Minitel-type terminals);
— communications authorities' policies in pricing conventional and electronic mail (and access to viewdata systems);
— efforts put into 'technology transfer' from business applications and from systems developed for marginalised groups such as handicapped people;[9]
— and the development of attractive services (which may be hastened by the international trade in such services, facilitated by the opening of access points in host countries).

Computer communications development would also, of course, be facilitated by improvements in consumer hardware. In the long run, we would expect to see the creation of portable computer-communications devices that combine many of the properties of telephones, calculators, data terminals, and display units (recall the discussion of the electronic newspaper above). One hint of this sort of development course is the portable teletext decoder that allows for convenient scanning of news and other broadcast teletext pages. And the development of the telephone itself, reviewed earlier, also moves in this direction.

4.8 Concluding notes

The evolution of telecommunications networks and services is and will continue to be a crucial determinant of the path of development taken by HI. Not surprisingly, perhaps, given the different experiences in different countries, whether telecommunications are seen as being the key to HI (information society as the 'telematic society', as is the case in France), or whether stand-alone equipment is the focus of attention (as seems to be more the case in Britain), can vary considerably. Given the pace of development in telecommunications networks, however, it is very likely that the interrelation of domestic equipment with these networks is bound to grow in importance everywhere—even where the pace of upgrading consumer connections to the PSTN or to cable services is slow.

The next chapter moves on to consider the process of innovation in consumer electronics. Some of the innovations here are competitive with telecommunications-based goods and services, but we shall also see that some are complementary. Furthermore, many common themes and issues run through these two chapters, despite the differences between the telecommunications and consumer electronics sectors. Thus we shall refrain from elaborating on these points—for example, the role of standards, shifts in market orientations of producers—until the end of Chapter 5.

Notes

1. The discussion in this section draws upon a number of sources, including *Business Week* (1983), Forester (1987), Hills (1986), Melody (1986), Snow and Jussawalla (1986), Tunstall (1986) and Tydeman and Kelm (1986). For one of a very few studies of developments in telecommunications (and consumer electronics) sectors that analyses policy developments within a political science framework, see Cawson *et al.* (1986).
2. Keller *et al.* (1986).
3. This perspective was formulated in the report of the Information Technology Advisory Panel (ITAP, 1982). For a French study of cable futures see CNET (1983).
4. Philips (1987) presents the case for MAC forcefully and glossily.
5. There is some confusion over terminology here, with national differences in nomenclature. Generally, 'Videotext' covers all page-based methods of displaying written information and basic graphics on VDUs; broadcast videotext is 'teletext', interactive videotext is 'videotex' or viewdata. We use viewdata here to avoid confusion, even though it is not universally familiar. Our discussion of viewdata draws on Kaye (1986) and presentations made at the Home Informatics workshop by Bourgoin on Teletel, Kappetyn (1986) on Ditzitel, and by Russel (1986) on Prestel; and on a series of interviews conducted by the author and Graham Thomas in 1987.
6. This was outlined by Serafina Cernusch Salkoff of the CNRS, Paris, in her presentation 'II Minitel-Dialogue per i non udenti' at the conference 'Nuove Technologie e Vita Quotidiana in Europa' in Bologna, November 1987.
7. Information Dynamics Limited (1986).
8. Iwaasa (1985, 1986).
9. See British Telecom (1985) for a representative sample of telephone innovations aimed at disabled customers.

5 Consumer electronics: brown goods and black boxes

5.1 A critical sector

North American and European consumer electronics industries have faced strong challenges from Japanese competition (and, more recently, from Newly Industrialising Countries in South East Asia, in particular South Korea). The manufacture of audio and monochrome TV equipment in Western Europe has declined substantially, and many firms have disappeared or joined large companies—who have tended to shift to goods like colour TV and VTRs.

This has given rise to considerable concern, for several reasons:

— consumer electronics is a sector that consumes locally produced components, and acts as a stimulus to manufacturers of these components in terms of technological innovation;
— consumer electronics is a sector intimately linked to entertainment services like broadcasting and recording;
— while small in terms of overall manufacturing output, and while subject to considerable rationalisation and labour-saving innovation in recent years, the sector is an important employer in some localities, and major firms have been seen as flagships of national technology.

Industrial policy for the consumer electronics sector has overlapped with cultural and mass media policy, given that the goods involved have in the main—home computers are the leading exception—been devices for distributing mass entertainment and news services. Furthermore, this is one of two sectors that have been considerably significant in the post-war reshaping of ways of life.

In the post-war period, two broad classes of consumer goods were associated with massive changes in way of life and economic structure in the industrial societies of the West. 'White goods' brought cheap motor power to households, reducing the effort required for many domestic work tasks and providing cheap and convenient alternatives to traditional services such as laundries. Also based on motor power and substituting for traditional (transport) services, the related innovation of the motor car (not usually classed as a white good!) is of most significance here, with the automobile industry being a key pillar of industrial growth[1]—certainly this has been associated with considerable change in urban form and the spatial structure of everyday life.

'Brown goods'[2]—based on the application of electronics innovations like thermionic valves, transistors and CRTs to consumer goods—were also important, but instead of permitting consumer self-servicing[3] (which required inputs of informal labour to achieve household ends), they typically changed the consumption of services. They allowed for new means of delivery of entertainment, news and related types of information to the consumer. Audio and video outputs through CRTs and loudspeakers substituted for some traditional services like cinema and theatre (and some print media), while also opening up new consumption markets.

Thus, traditional consumer electronics (radios, TVs, record players and tape recorders), together with the complementary information services (broadcasting and recording), have mainly been used by consumers to satisfy requirements for entertainment. This entertainment function is often used to achieve other ends, and not merely for relaxation, stimulation or leisure. For example, parents may set children to watch TV in order to reduce the load of childcare (especially when the streets are rendered unsafe for children by automobile traffic). Ethnographic research demonstrates, too, that in some families TV viewing is used as a way of controlling social interactions ('don't disturb father, he's watching his favourite programme').

In addition to, and often in tandem with, the entertainment function, broadcast services in particular provide 'intelligence' functions by supplying news, travel information, etc. There have been relatively minor applications of gramophone records and tape recording for less time-critical applications such as language tuition, and distance learning schemes (in the case of the latter, the students often record programmes broadcast at awkward hours, for their subsequent use). Both entertainment and 'intelligence' functions are bound to remain important, and may be augmented in order to make them more realistic, more interactive, more tailored to individual characteristics and circumstances; additionally, new consumer electronic goods (especially those involving computer-communications) may increasingly assist other types of function—education, social intercourse, producing as well as simply relaying information (e.g. health monitoring, household security, music synthesis and interior ambience, etc.). Let us consider specific classes of 'brown goods'.

5.2 TV-related electronics

Mackintosh (1984) graphically illustrates the trends occurring over a very short period of time (1975–82) in European Community TV markets. Over the period there was a decline in the consumption of monochrome TVs (from 5.6 million to 3.7 million per annum); but, of that, the non-EEC import share grew from 23 to 56 per cent (with non-Japanese Far East producers growing from 7 to 37 per cent). The colour TV market—accounting for around two-thirds of consumer expenditure—grew from 5.5 to 10.5 million units, with non-EEC imports growing from 12 to 18 per cent. VCR sales were negligible

Table 5.1 Video cassette recorders in Western Europe

Country	Estimated penetration			Formats in use		
	1981	1984	1990	VHS	Betamax	V2000
Austria	2:2	5.0	23	30	10	60
Belgium	4.4	5.9	29	70	25	5
Denmark	3.8	10.4	27	64	26	10
Finland	0.9	4.6	21	70	20	5
France	2.3	6.0	32	81	13	6
Fed. Rep. Germany	7.0	18.1	44	48	18	34
Ireland	—	9.8	32	75	15	10
Italy	0.3	2.0	9	60	25	15
Netherlands	—	7.7	34	55	25	20
Norway	6.4	15.7	37	80	13	7
Spain	1.3	12.7	19	40	50	10
Sweden	8.4	14.7	39	78	8	14
Switzerland	—	6.8	21	70	10	20
United Kingdom	7.6	28.1	49	70	22	8

Source: Tables 7.1, 7.2 from Tydeman and Kelm (1986), originally derived from several sources.

in the mid-1970s (a Philips machine had been launched in 1971), but by 1982 the market was 4.7 million units, of which 92 per cent were imported, and accounted for a rapidly growing share of consumer expenditure. (See Table 5.1 for trends in VCR use across Western Europe more generally.)

The role of technical standards has been of great importance in this field of consumer electronics. The production of video images is a complicated business, with various incompatible formats available for producing an intelligible and realistic picture on the screen (or for storing the relevant signals on tape or disc).

In the case of colour TV, most European countries adopted the PAL broadcasting standard; Canada, Japan and the United States had earlier adopted the (technically inferior) NTSC system. PAL was developed in West Germany by Telefunken and cross-licenced to Thorn in the United Kingdom. Imports of TVs from outside Europe were then restricted by means of selective licensing to Far East TV manufacturers, limiting their sales to Europe (many other countries had also adopted PAL). This has enabled European manufacturers to achieve competitive volumes and prices of production. France's SECAM system (adopted by some Eastern bloc countries and ex-French colonies) has also tended to insulate the French market further. This 'passive protectionism' may now be threatened by the availability of multi-standard TV chassis; but perhaps it established an image of a golden age of European consumer electronics that is still behind some of the enthusiasm for MAC and other non-Japanese standards.[4]

In the case of VCRs, in contrast to that of TV, European standards—in the shape of Philips' V2000, as opposed to Japanese Betamax and VHS standards—have been relatively unsuccessful. V2000 was introduced jointly by Philips and the German firm Grundig, but failed to gain support from other large European manufacturers, who chose to favour VHS (for reasons of rivalry with Philips and Grundig?). It has achieved relatively high penetration into German- and Dutch-speaking countries: according to Tydeman and Kelm (1986) this involved some 60 per cent of Austrian and 54 per cent of West German units in the mid-1980s, and a considerable proportion of units installed in the Netherlands and Switzerland. But in other European countries the share is less than 10 per cent, and worldwide VHS appears to be increasingly dominant. VTR imports from the Far East have thus been important, and the rapid growth of the market has led to protectionist moves in Europe and North America—the most famous of which was the French decision that VCRs being imported should be inspected by customs in a small office at Poitiers (with attendant publicity as a huge pile of items grew alongside the customs shed). One result has been inward investment and licensing from Japan for European manufacture. Three-quarters of the European plants manufacturing VCRs were producing according to VHS or Betamax standards by 1983 (Mackintosh International, 1984).

It should also be noted that Philips (and RCA in the United States) was associated with an alternative means of storing video images, the videodisc system. Despite the high standards of reproduction that videodiscs made possible, they faltered when confronted by the market challenge of VTRs (rather as viewdata often ran into awkward competition from the parallel innovation of teletext). The main disadvantage of videodiscs was the inability of consumers to record their own selections on the discs: they were forced to buy or rent programmes, and while videotape shops have been a booming retail sector, the opportunity to time-shift has also been a significant part of the attraction of VTRs. Launched in Europe in 1982 as a consumer item, by the mid-1980s the main market for videodisc systems was a business one, as their potential for training and promotional use became clear. The usefulness of *interactive* videodisc in these applications provided Philips with a lesson that has been incorporated in the development of interactive Compact Disc (CD-I) systems (and similarly by RCA in its proposals for the somewhat similar DVI system). We shall discuss these in the next subsection; first we should consider recent developments in TV electronics.

The issue of standards has become prominent in the lively—not to say furious—debates that have gone on around HDTV (High Definition TV). HDTV systems will deliver TV images of extremely high quality as compared to current technology. Watson Brown (1987) describes the emergence of a coalition of European interests that (temporarily) blocked a Japanese proposal, backed by the United States, to adopt Japanese HDTV standards. The European Community played a significant role in mobilising these European interests, setting up meetings and information exchanges to alert civil servants, broadcasters and manufacturers to what was seen as a substantial threat.

The Japanese HDTV proposals represent a quantum step in TV systems. Immensely improved image quality (over 1100 lines on the screen, as compared to the current European 625-line TV, with more 'samples' per line for luminescence and colour difference, giving clearer and more realistic pictures) is attained by a route that involves new camera and studio equipment, new broadcasting systems, and new receivers. Complacent electronics industries around the world were surprised by the rapid technical progress made towards this system in Japan, and US standards bodies and entertainment industries were won over to it. European firms had been working on a less radical upgrading of existing TV systems, whereby existing technologies would be compatible with the HDTV equipment and services. The relative neglect of consumer electronics as an area for industrial strategy delayed recognition that extremely large markets would essentially be ceded by adoption of the Japanese HDTV standard.

At the time of writing, the situation remains confused. The Europeans have to cooperate among themselves to establish a viable counter-proposal for HDTV standards. A large sum of money has been committed to this process, which is one of the projects funded as part of the Eureka programme. It does appear that HDTV standards are being treated as a global issue rather than just as a means of protecting regional markets. Detailed standards have been elaborated, based on 1250-line pictures and a rapid 'screen refresh' which gives a flickerless picture, and the thirty firms cooperating in the Eureka project demonstrated a HDTV system in Berlin in autumn 1987.

Despite these signs of progress, and the fairly convincing rationale provided for the superiority of the European proposals in many respects, this may be seen as eleventh-hour activity; the ability of Europe to secure competitive advantage—or even some measure of competitive equality—remains uncertain. Japanese suppliers have achieved considerable inroads in winning the European cinema industry towards high-definition video (according to Japanese standards) as a framework for future movie production (RAI studios in Milan are notable exponents of this), and are proposing beginning DBS HDTV transmissions in 1990—before European systems are in mass production. Super VHS, a new VCR development from the JVC company, which considerably improves the quality of video recordings, can also be seen as consolidating Japan's lead in upgraded TV.

HDTV makes a fascinating, if alarming, case study of the issues surrounding HI. In particular, the revolutionary versus evolutionary approaches to establishing HDTV clearly intersect the issues of consumer acceptance discussed in Chapter 3. Will the advantages of HDTV be sufficient to support a change to new broadcasting systems? What will be the behaviour of corporate actors—cable and broadcasting companies and film-makers among them? Whatever the outcome of these developments proves to be, the HDTV case is worth watching closely: it demonstrates rather starkly the economic (and cultural) significance of HI, and its relative neglect in strategic thinking to date—except, presumably, in Japan.

5.3 Future TV

Chapter 2 outlined trends in consumer electronics goods, many of which are particularly relevant to TV. Thus, improved control and display features have been pioneered in consumer electronics goods. Given that the function of entertainment supplied by these goods is heavily dependent on the quality of their output, it is not surprising that much innovative effort in product development centres on improving these outputs. While even quite small loudspeakers are now able to emulate real-life sound remarkably well, the TV screen clearly has a way to go before its images can be mistaken for reality. Three-dimensional TV is not on the immediate horizon, and even though several likely-looking technologies are under development, the 'software' for such systems may be a long time in coming. But several significant developments are likely in the TV screen in the next few years (together with associated developments in reception apparatus): see Table 5.2.

In addition to improvements in the screen itself, stereo sound TV sets are now on the market (indeed, suppliers have been annoyed in Britain by the BBC's surprise announcement in 1987 that it will *not* consider stereo broadcasts for several more years). As well as providing high-quality audio output (which could be reproduced through one's stereo system), the ability to separate sound channels also offers the prospect of using one channel for bilingual broadcasts (e.g. simultaneous reception of original *and* dubbed versions, or French and Walloon versions, of a film) or for emergency information and messaging functions (peritelevision).

Perhaps the most important development in TV will be the establishment of digital TV systems. These are based on the decoding of digitalised broadcasts: it is anticipated that their pictures will be freer from interference. Furthermore, such TVs can more readily incorporate new functions such as the ability to store pictures, to output pictures or text to printers, to allow viewers to operate 'windows' or split screens (so that one can check the contents of other channels without leaving that currently viewed), to manipulate images (e.g. enlarge portions of the screen), and to selectively tune into specific programmes or to override programmes to carry emergency messages. Some of these functions are being introduced into new TV models, which offer some digital processing of signals originally received in analogue form. Many of them clearly represent a step towards greater interactivity of domestic equipment.

The transition to fully digitalised TV is likely to be a slow one since the transmission systems involved are substantially different from those now in use, raising problems of reverse compatibility. Moralee (1985) suggests that all-digital standards are unlikely to be adopted until the late 1990s.

Table 5.2   Developments in the television screen

● *'Flat'*, *or rather thin, TV screens*, suitable for hanging on walls or incorporating into control panels. Such screens can be used in settings where space is at a premium (e.g. small kitchens, car dashboards . . . and pockets and briefcases). While several technologies are being pursued, most effort is currently being devoted to Liquid Crystal Display systems.

● *Low-power-consuming screens*. Flat-screen technology is typically much more economical in the use of electricity than CRT, and thus the usefulness of portable screens is increased. There is also more scope for new applications of video screens, so that, for example, high-quality graphics produced by home computers or CD-I systems, or 'video art' such as has already been exposed in several galleries, may be displayed in place of conventional pictures (or even in place of wallpaper).

● *'Widescreen' TV*. While there is considerable international debate over standards for systems permitting video displays some twice as wide as those now current, and this may delay acceptance of new systems, some form of widescreen HDTV is likely to be in place by the mid-1990s.

● *'High-definition' TV*. Yielding pictures with quality approaching that of 35mm photography, this might also facilitate new applications of the VDU. For example, together with electronic cameras this might lead to new types of photograph album, together with CD-I to new types of art book, together with widescreen TV to large (wall-sized?) screens and projection TV.

Already some digital broadcasts are employed as a means for the transmission of 'peripheral' information alongside conventional broadcasts. Teletext TV is already familiar, as we saw in Chapter 4—millions of teletext-equipped sets have been sold in Western Europe. The digital nature of this system is apparent from the effects of bad reception: instead of a degraded image, mistakes are made in the decoding of portions of the text. The teletext TV set is a standard one equipped with a special teletext chip: it remains capable of accessing conventional broadcasts. There has been some doubt expressed concerning how far teletext is actually used by owners of teletext-equipped sets: market research suggests that the main users are young, well-educated men, and that the most popular uses are for current information rather than entertainment.

It seems practically certain that digital broadcasting will develop in parallel to conventional analogue broadcasts, just as FM radio has emerged alongside AM systems (which still remain lively, despite the superior quality and stereo capabilities of FM). Digitalisation is likely to favour the continued integration of home entertainment systems: as TV is able to broadcast high-quality stereo sound, for example, this may be increasingly output through the hi-fi system, and there may be some 'blending' of materials derived from different media. (For example, in one of John Brunner's novels—published as long ago as 1969!—a system is invoked whereby the TV presenter appears to address the viewer by name, and images of the viewer in the scenes depicted are 'pasted' seamlessly onto the screen).

Digitalisation also makes some data compression techniques more readily applicable, and thus supports HDTV systems, and a proliferation of channels. But the substantial increase in the pictorial quality and quantitative choice of TV programmes requires high bandwidth media. Direct Broadcast Satellite vies with cable TV to perform this role.

DBS has advantages in being able to serve remote and inaccessible areas. With more powerful receivers attached to satellite dishes, it also becomes possible to draw upon broadcasts aimed at very distant regions, which may appeal to dispersed ethnic communities (who now support an international flow of videotapes). Objections to the extensive use of satellite dishes in urban areas on the grounds of the unsightliness of large dishes, and simple financial obstacles to the proliferation of expensive dishes and decoders, may be expected to become less significant as substantial reductions in cost and size of dishes are achieved. Increasingly the barriers to DBS will be national policies and the cost of the broadcast services.

Cable installation is certainly not inexpensive, though there are economies of scale. It can make possible the 'personalisation' of TV transmission—a shift from broadcasting to 'narrowcasting'. (Thus, on one cable system in the United Kingdom, it is already possible for users to choose from broadcasts taking place elsewhere in the world, or to view selections from a range of videodiscs as if they were on a domestic video recorder, with the capability of slowing and freezing the picture, of speeding up or reversing the display.) Perhaps most importantly, for the development of new consumer services, broadband cable can provide the infrastructural basis for a range of such services additional to TV transmission. (We consider the scope for new services in a later subsection.) In the long term, an optical fibre cable-based telecommunications infrastructure seems the most likely model, and some national governments are already promoting this; but in many cases neither the PTTs nor the cable TV operators seem particularly keen on taking the gamble of installing new systems while it remains unclear that sufficient latent demand for new services exists.

What does this discussion imply for the organisation of video display equipment in the home? A number of conclusions can be drawn:

— It is likely that the TV screen will become more important as a vehicle for information flows into the household and perhaps around the home—in coming years.
— The TV screen will be not only a medium for the display of prepackaged information products; it will also be used as the interface for interactive

products (games, as an 'electronic blackboard' or 'easel', etc.).
— However, this does not mean that the 'home of the future' will necessarily be oriented around a specialised home entertainments or data room, as often depicted by futurologists. It is possible that living rooms may contain massive screens, although LCD technologies will need to progress some way for really large screens to be achieved. But these screens will probably not be allowed to dominate the room, at least not once they have been given prominence as status symbols. Rather, methods of allowing them to blend into the ambience—perhaps as imitation windows or electronic wallpaper—will probably be sought.
— In contrast, the availability of small, thin, cheap VDUs will probably lead to a proliferation of screens in the home. Some will be dedicated to specific purposes (entertainment, displaying household information), others will be used in a multifunctional manner (as computer screens, video game displays, peritelevision, etc.). The two-TV home is not infrequent at present and it is likely that, just as cheap transistor radios have led to many households possessing several radios (a music centre, a personal stereo receiver, a car radio, a portable radio for the children, and so on), so cheap TVs and VDUs will promote the multi-screen home. (Many British homes acquired their second TV set in order to free the living room TV, and/or the living room itself, from the children's games on a home computer; but as newer home computers provide better-quality displays than those cheap TVs can cope with, dedicated VDUs look to be the immediate trend.)

5.4 Radio

The most obvious—some would say most intrusive—developments in radio systems in recent years have been associated with the development of personal stereos (typically combining radio and audio tape facilities, and criticised on the grounds that they are anything but 'personal' to those forced to share, say, a train carriage with the user) and, to a lesser extent, car radios. There has been a steady decline in the audio manufacturing sectors in Europe and North America as Far East manufacturers have moved into cheap and innovative products (the personal stereo was first produced by Sony of Japan).

It remains to be seen whether the radio equivalent to teletext, Radio Data Services (RDS), will provide a new opportunity for European manufacturers. It is certainly clear that the European Broadcasting Union and some national broadcasting authorities have been actively working on standards for RDS, which we will describe shortly. However, Japanese radio manufacturers are already well-established in the field of digital tuning on radio systems (allowing for automatic search for optimum reception of a particular channel), and competition from this quarter must be anticipated.

What are Radio Data Services? In many respects, as mentioned, these are radio equivalents of teletext. RDS would enable equipped radios to display information on programme content and the channel currently being relayed, to search for specific types of programme or a specific channel (or the best signal for a given channel), to override the channel being used to broadcast emergency messages, etc. While digitalised radio broadcasts face many of the same problems of compatibility as digital TV, and are thus likely to appeal in the first instance to hi-fi enthusiasts, RDS are currently being introduced in several countries, to transmit data on the station involved (and subsequently on the content of various programmes—the European Broadcasting Union has agreed identification codes that can indicate whether news, light music, or other classes of material are being broadcast), and to convey emergency information. Even partly digital receivers are enabled to tune in to a particular station, searching across the radio spectrum for the frequency that gives the best reception. (This is particularly useful when one is travelling in a motor vehicle, when reception quality is liable to vary from transmitter to transmitter.) Similarly, these receivers will be able to override a programme to transmit emergency warnings or traffic and weather information; some radios will turn themselves on when such material is broadcast.

Again, motorists are seen as a particularly significant target audience, requiring up-to-date warnings of traffic conditions and roadworks. RDS here interrelates with the CD-I systems which we describe later: Philips plan for future models of their Carin CD-based electronic map for drivers to be able to determine appropriate routes and route alterations, taking account of RDS broadcasts.[5]

Future uses of RDS include being able to instruct a radio to search for a given type of programme, or to turn itself or else recording apparatus on when a particular broadcast begins; and the display of 'radiotext' on a small screen attached to the receiver. Similar services associated with TV broadcasts are under development so that, for example, it is possible for a 'smart' VTR to commence recording when a particular programme begins. (But will it be able to skip the advertisements?) As experience with the uses and users of such services grows, and as digital receivers become available, and themselves undergo further product development, further development of such systems, and their use to supply more services, is highly likely.

Some confusion is probably being created for consumers by the uneven progress of digitalisation. For example, the first generation of 'digital radios' that became available in the mid- and late 1980s really only featured digital tuning and display. This makes them more user-friendly, and particularly useful for disabled people; but it does not involve the reception of digital broadcasts. But, in general, the trend towards the digitalisation of the functions of consumer electronics is bound to be a central axis for many further innovations in both goods and associated services. The superior quality of their performance means that digital audio and videotape recorders, for example, are likely to challenge existing systems—as European defenders of the CD industry fear will be the case for DAT.

5.5. CD systems

Japanese producers have also made significant inroads into hi-fi markets, although there are many niches for specialised quality producers here. The most significant development in this field is the audio CD, whose diffusion has exceeded market forecasts (and revitalised the record retailing sector). Based on Philips research, CD players were developed collaboratively by Philips and Sony, and were first marketed in 1981—since when costs of the players (though not the discs) have fallen rapidly. Other firms adopted the Philips–Sony standard, and record companies have produced considerable volumes of discs (though demand outstrips supply); Japanese consumer electronics manufacturers are dominant in the field, but have been accused of dumping CD players in Europe (where their prices are allegedly well below Japanese levels), as have South Korean manufacturers. (Japanese and South Korean CD players are estimated to account for two-thirds of the European market—not surprisingly since their prices are below those of European models.)

By the mid-1980s, CD systems were also becoming available as a mass data storage system for microcomputers—CD-ROM. (This was in addition to their large-scale diffusion as a home audio product—over ten million CD players had been sold by late 1986.) The role of standards was again substantial here, since it was recognised that it would be of great importance to the rapid diffusion of CD-ROM to business users if discs and drives from different manufacturers were to be compatible. In late 1985 the High Sierra group was formed by hardware and software firms (including Apple, DEC, Hitachi, Philips and Sony) and rapidly prepared a specification for standards. In parallel, Philips and Sony developed a CD-I standard that would be able to read CD-ROM data. In autumn 1987 Sony was demonstrating a CD-I system publicly in Japan: hi-fi music from a rock band is accompanied by text, animation, still pictures and brief snatches of video, with a menu that allows viewers to choose what to see and hear. Sony sees the video games market as a likely user of CD-I, since it offers interactivity together with realism.

Turner (1986b) has outlined Philips' strategy to build upon the rapid diffusion of CD and CD-ROM, and establish CD-I as a new mass market. The aim is to achieve agreement on international standards for new applications of CD that would be fully compatible with existing audio and data standards, and allow new applications to build upon the diffusion of audio CD devices. CD-I systems would be capable of simply replaying audio (and basic graphics) material in a linear fashion, but would also allow for interactive uses. Examples include: reference-book type access to encyclopaedia, dictionary and handbook text, illustrations and audio (e.g. pronunciation guides in dictionaries), visual and audio image sources for new types of computer-assisted painting and music synthesis, video games, etc.

Philips anticipates large consumer and institutional markets for such devices, and is thus pressing hard for agreement on standards so that all CD-I discs will play on all CD-I players. The question of standards is emerging as an important point of dispute in the electronic publishing industry, with some sources claiming, and others denying, that CD-I is merely a promotional gimmick to dress up CD-ROM.[6] In early 1987 Philips surprised many observers and critics by unveiling a CD video (CD-V) system, able to store five minutes of video imagery with accompanying sound and a further twenty minutes of hi-fi: players retailing for around £500 are expected to appeal particularly to the pop video market. (Though at present suppliers of the appropriate 'software' seem to be adopting a 'wait-and-see' attitude rather than rushing to supply material for CD-V). However, the video images are recorded in analogue form (like earlier videodiscs, but using a somewhat different technical standard) rather than as digital signals, and thus represent a step away from the digital technological trajectory of CD audio and CD-ROM and towards a 'hybrid' technology.

Meanwhile, RCA in the United States announced Digital Video Interactive (DVI), an approach to data compression allowing for over an hour's video on a CD—a development that may undermine CD-I through the conflict of standards. But DVI requires new, advanced decompression equipment. CD-V, in contrast, utilises established videodisc technology, and Philips are exploring options for converting or allowing trade-ins of videodisc systems.[7] Innovation researchers might well explore the parallels between the strategies embodied in these two video systems—one allowing for use of existing equipment, one requiring completely new equipment—and the two HDTV systems discussed earlier; again we see a quantum leap pitted against an incremental strategy, although in this case a new, rather than an improved, product is involved. Whether one strategy is clearly superior, whether both will become established, or whether the competition between systems inhibits market development, is yet to become clear. But we can be fairly sure that some consumer technology utilising IT to provide interactive 'hypermedia' is likely to become familiar over the next decade.

Before we move on to consider the possible uses for CD-I or similar systems, other developments in digital audio that pose questions for CD development should be noted. First are new forms of CD: for example, in early 1987 it was reported that technical standards and marketing aspects of mini-compact discs were being discussed by Philips and Sony. Disagreements were reported between the two companies: while smaller discs would permit smaller players, there would be problems of establishing adaptors for conventional players to play mini-discs, and in possibly confusing consumers over competing music devices.[8]

Second is the launch of DAT, digital audio tape systems, in 1987, by several Japanese firms—Aiwa, Matsushita, Sony and Toshiba. (Philips is also developing DAT systems, and plans to manufacture them in Japan using Japanese components; Grundig has also announced plans to make and sell DAT in Europe.) DAT brings digitalisation to home audio recording, though players are currently expensive and rather bulky (unlike the tapes themselves.) American and European concerns about DAT are twofold. There is fear that the fledgling CD and CD player industries will be undermined by consumers preferring DAT systems. And the superior copying capabilities of DAT raise fears that CDs and LPs will be 'pirated'. In the United States and the EEC this latter threat has led to pressure for DATs to incorporate 'spoilers' which inhibit copying: Japanese companies have expressed reluctance to agree to this, as have some music specialists and consumers, but Philips is prepared to go along with this. Clearly, a non-tariff trade barrier may be created here. Five leading record companies have stated that they will not allow their music to be released on DAT unless 'spoilers' are incorporated: the hope is that the threat of lack of software will change hardware manufacturers' minds. (During the period of revision of this text, one of these companies, CBS, has subsequently been bought by Sony, while Sony has also agreed to incorporate a spoiler in the DAT systems it has begun to sell in Britain: watch this space!)

As with HDTV standards, this is currently a lively and contentious area. The record company CBS has claimed that its Copycode system is an adequate safeguard against audio piracy. The international Federation of Phonogram and Videogram Producers, supporting this, has asked the European Commission and the US government to make it mandatory for DAT recorders to have inbuilt Copycode circuits, which would recognise 'protected' recordings. However, Fox (1987b) reports that in US and UK trials in 1987, music specialists claimed that the Copycode system (involving a 'notch' in the audio frequency spectrum) actually degrades sound quality.

With digital amplifiers (and radio receivers) being logical extensions of the CD and DAT developments, it seems likely that consumer audio products will continue to attract considerable interest in international trade affairs in coming years. While audio CD and CD-ROM have so far demonstrated the possibilities of rapid market expansion given agreement on standards, the disputes that are emerging around CD-I are possibly indicative of turmoil ahead around new consumer products.

5.6 Mass data storage as consumer technology

Mass data storage, traditionally a concern of mainframe and minicomputer users, is now becoming of significance to owners of personal computers; and soon it is liable to be important for HI. But, just as Minitel terminals may not be considered as home computers (while utilising computer-communications prospects), so CD-I systems may not be recognised as home computers. This may be an advantage in marketing terms: they can be sold as devices providing useful services rather than as gadgets to be purchased for their own sake. If CD-I systems retailing at little more than the cost of standard items of audio and video equipment become available in the late 1980s, they may well not be marketed as an improved home computer, but rather as a new type of domestic utility: the idea is that home computers' image has been tarnished by the lack of useful applications.

The ultimate success of the system will depend upon the variety, quality and costs of the informational material available on CDs. Quite possibly this will be a technology where the mass market is developed through a number of 'trigger sectors'—car owners, parents concerned about educational provisions, etc. In the longer-term, video disc systems and/or improvement in other methods of data storage promise to make available even more massive volumes of information—the Domesday Project developed for British schools is only an early indication of this.

Some CD-I systems may be devoted to specific purposes. One of these is the music video player, as suggested by Philips' CD-V system. Another special-purpose application is the Carin car-based CD which stores road maps and gives route advice, and perhaps will eventually be able to convey data on hospitality and sites of special interest *en route* (possibly linked to computer-communications as well as RDS). But this example also hints at the multi-purpose nature of CD: for a car CD-I system could additionally be used for in-car music. (The CD-ROM system to be released in 1988 for the Atari ST—at an estimated cost of £400—will be able to play audio CDs.)

CD-I may be sold through specific applications aimed at 'trigger audiences'. But it is a prime example of the multifunctionality of emerging computer/data storage technologies. And although we have argued that future HI markets are more likely to be structured around services than around the technologies that can deliver them, the fact that a system can be used for several distinct, attractive types of application can only count in its favour. The types of application likely with CD-I are listed in Table 5.3.[9]

One limitation of CD systems currently available is their ROM—read-only-nature. WORM, 'write once-read many times' systems, are becoming available for business users, permitting some new data entry. At some point prices of this technology will fall to consumer levels; meanwhile, completely rewriteable systems are forecast to be on the market by the early 1990s.) This may not be significant for many of the domestic applications cited in Table 5.3; there is no reason why a ROM mass data storage system should not be coupled with some more familiar storage system for consumer entry. Alternatively, DAT or VTR systems may provide the basis for mass data storage, but are less suitable for interactive applications (owing to the problem of rapidly moving from one point to another on the tape).

We should not let the high level of enthusiasm being expressed blind us to alternative data storage/display technologies. One of the dreams of IT developers has been the development of alternatives to the book, and the idea

Table 5.3   Illustrative consumer applications of interactive optical media

- Familiar audio and video applications involving access to recorded music and still or moving pictures in a more or less linear fashion (CD-audio, CD-V).
- More interactive audio and video applications, such as 'elastic music' (providing the ability to rescore given compositions, to play them with different selections of instruments, etc.), electronic picture albums and 'wallpaper' designs.
- Electronic dictionaries, with illustrations and examples of pronunciation (useful in multilingual dictionaries), and search facilities unavailable on any printed dictionaries.
- Electronic encyclopedias.
- Databases for DIY menus and other housework that benefits from informational inputs, maps for route planning, etc., and information on fittings and decoration which can be used for the application of Computer-Aided Design facilities to room planning, etc.
- New types of artistic tool, such as music synthesisers or VDU-based graphic art devices.
- Media for the display of directories, shopping catalogues, consumer advice, etc.

of an electronic notepad, magic slate, or 'Dynabook' has been around for a long time. One of the key attractions of this sort of system is the possibility of competing with books by offering a lightweight and portable device, one that is easily readable, but which can accommodate interactive functions.

A step on the way to this was announced in 1987: an Australian firm announced the 'Smartbook', which stores text on a 'chip' (so far only the Bible is available, cleverly compressed into less than a megabyte of ROM) and displays it on a reader with a 15 x 20cm screen (which displays, in addition to the text, a menu line from which options may be chosen using a six-key keyboard). The system should make it easy to carry or store informationally large but physically small volumes of reading material. These can be read, 'marked', subjected to concordance analysis, etc.; future systems are anticipated to feature large screens (e.g. for library use, colour screens, printers, etc.). Whether this particular system proves successful or not, IT-based competitors to books are bound to be produced and eventually to achieve market shares. They may even be CD-I based, since three-inch CDs are under development and portable CD players are already little bigger than personal stereos.

In the shorter term, a significant factor in the evolution of storage technologies for HI is the coevolution of data storage and telecommunications. In some instances this may involve competition between the different modes of supplying data to end-users. Why should consumers choose either a CD or an online service, for example, for specific information? The answer will depend very much upon the user requirements for information:

— How topical is it? Does the data need to be up to date, like traffic information or retail prices, or need they be only infrequently refreshed, like menus or DIY tips?

— What level of quality is needed? Even photographic-quality pictures take considerable time to be delivered via conventional telephone wires, but CD-I can only provide relatively short moving video sequences; in contrast a broadband cable system can supply HDTV-quality displays.

— And, of course, what costs is the user prepared to pay, and what level of convenience is required? Among the latter features, for example, are the portability of the output devices, the reliability and availability of the data, and the range of services available via competing modes of delivery of data.

But quite possibly the relation between the two modes of delivery of data will be characterised by complementarity rather than competition. The development of HI may facilitate a parallel growth of both data storage and data communications technologies. Rather than how they compete in overall terms, the interesting question may really be how the two types of system intermesh for specific applications—how their technological and market trajectories affect each other.

Indeed, CD-I may turn out to be the turnkey domestic technology that first applies computer power to useful purposes in large numbers of ordinary households. If this is the case, it might then be providing the HI equipment which consumers may subsequently link to telecommunications networks. Just as the Carin in-car route-finding CD-I system may be using Radio Data Services to improve its usefulness by avoiding traffic jams, so other applications may combine mass data storage with telecommunications. To take a teleshopping example, if the broadband infrastructure is not in place to allow one to inspect items as they are held in the shop, perhaps the quality pictures of items could be delivered on a CD shopping catalogue, while information on current prices, availability, delivery schedules, etc. could be obtained interactively via computer-communications.

5.7 Home computers

Home computers first emerged in the United States as a hobbyist interest in the mid-1970s, with self-assembly kits being marketed by MITS Inc. and IMS Associates Inc. A surprisingly large consumer market developed, so that by 1977 around fifty suppliers served perhaps 30,000 users—mostly professionals with some work-based interest in computing.[10] Apple is a notable company emerging in this period.

The first explosion of a non-professional, mass consumer market was apparent in the United Kingdom in the early 1980s. This was prompted by the first really cheap machine (the Sinclair ZX80 at less than £100), and by media attention to IT. Sinclair was soon producing over one million units per annum, and was joined by a large number of other small firms (mainly in the United Kingdom and the United States). Over twenty models were on the British market by the end of 1983, few of which survived in the retail sector by early 1987 (although a handful of these were available in substantially upgraded and generally cheaper versions). [11] It was 1985 that was the year of shake-out in both home and business microcomputer markets, with many of the new producers and retailers going out of business or having to substantially reorient their activities. The main Sinclair machines were sold off to the consumer electronics firm Amstrad. Amstrad has been one of the few consumer electronics firms to successfully move into home computer production; it has more recently pioneered cheap word processing computers for home/small business use.

The United Kingdom is still believed to have the highest per capita home computer ownership in the world: estimates of the proportion of households owning a computer range from 15 to 25 per cent. (But note that around 25 per cent of Japanese families possess a Famicon, Nintendo's very cheap—less than $100—video games computer, which can be upgraded for computer communications even though it does not possess a keyboard. [12] And also consider that many home computers may not really be used any more: unlike the telephone or Minitel terminal, they are rather readily put into a cupboard and forgotten.) As hinted above, the home computers diffused in Britain and other countries will vary from very basic machines—perhaps even some remaining 1k Sinclair ZX80s, certainly many 16k and 32k machines—to machines with processing power in excess of many business microcomputers, for example the 512k Acorn Master, the 1 (and now 4) megabyte Atari ST.

At the peak of the home computer boom in the mid-1980s, Japanese electronics manufacturers released a range of models onto European and American markets. For a variety of reasons these failed to gain a very substantial foothold; poor marketing and relatively little software were part of the story, but these machines were also not outstanding technically. However, one element of the Japanese strategy received considerable attention: the computers were technically compatible in that they supported the same software, MSX. In contrast, few of the models manufactured by companies in other Western countries would support each other's software —with the exception of the IBM PC-compatible microcomputers, at this point in time almost entirely a business market—and it was quite common to find that successive machines released by one manufacturer would be incompatible. For example, Sinclair's ZX80/81, Spectrum and QL machines were not compatible, which in part accounts for the market failure of the technically advanced QL. In principle, standardisation around MSX would present economies of scale in software production and distribution. But, in practice, the attractiveness of software available for established home computers outweighed this: MSX received inadequate support from the numerous software houses producing games and applications for home computers.

The situation has not yet stabilised following the 1985 shake-out, and the probable trend is towards new forms of market segmentation. In particular, a large number of cheap IBM-compatible machines were released or announced in 1986 and 1987. Firms like Atari and Amstrad have set out to undercut or at least equal the prices of South Korean and Taiwanese manufacturers, and to establish new markets among small businesses and home-based professionals.

Thus the distinction between home computer and business microcomputer has become blurred, and this may in part account for the reported drop in home computer sales: people were moving up to machines more adequate for professional use. But it is clear that these new models are not (at first, at any rate) primarily being sold for the entertainment and games functions that they nevertheless include. Rather, their markets, at least in the early stages, are based on a (limited) range of practical professional and semi-professional applications such as word processing, databases, spreadsheets, etc. (If a machine becomes well-established, however, then a flood of games and entertainment software may follow, and the nature of its market may thus change.) Computer hobbyists are being lured with technically advanced machines like the Apple Mackintosh, Commodore Amiga and Atari ST which, while not being IBM-compatible, still have the full range of business applications (and are actually more advanced in areas like Desk Top Publishing). These do support sophisticated video games, and such software is now produced on a large scale. There is also still a sizeable market for home computers where games are central—other Commodore and Atari machines, Sinclair machines, etc.—and even one for video game consoles (of which more sophisticated models are being launched, the earlier and more primitive models having been successfully challenged by the first home computers).

Yet another consumer market is the 'educational' one—for example, Acorn in the United Kingdom promote their computers as being similar to those used by children at school (where Acorn machines are dominant), thus enabling both parents and children to extend studies at home. Part of the reason for the early take-off of the UK home computer market was surely the belief that one's children needed computer skills to keep up with the competition in information society—and, at the same time, enthusiastic promotion of an ideology of self-help (rather than promises that the Welfare State would adequately educate children). Children certainly benefited from the computers, at least in so far as they were able to play games: the quality of educational software for home users was not notably good, although a proportion of children were certainly able to teach themselves impressive (if often ideosyncratic and undisciplined) programming skills.

5.8 Developing patterns of computer use

As we have seen, the industry shake-out in the home computer sector of the mid-1980s prompted manufacturers to revise their approach to marketing equipment. Among the more sophisticated consumers are those that have been particularly targeted by firms like Amstrad (and, to some extent, Atari and Apple, and Commodore with its Amiga). These firms have produced home/office computers for professional and semi-professional users, especially for those with small businesses based at home, or whose (usually professional) work is readily transportable between home and office. These home computers are used for word processing mainly, although other office applications seem to be growing in prominence. This type of use is likely to grow considerably, as consumer electronics manufacturers have realised that their skills in marketing and packaging equipment can be applied to mass markets for straightforward work-related word processor/home computer systems.

The segmentation of the home computer market—between more work- and more entertainment-oriented machines—is likely to persist even though, as microprocessor power grows, both types of machine are becoming capable of running either advanced word processing (spreadsheets, databases, etc.) or high-level video games (and other entertainment applications—such as music synthesis). It is also quite possible that software innovations will continue to favour different types of machine with different types of peripheral, such as a games machine with high-quality graphics and 'sprites' and a joystick—a work machine with easy-to-read screen, text displays and 'mouse'. Indeed, there is even speculation that the video games console, apparently rendered obsolete by more powerful home computers, will make a come-back, incorporating relatively up-to-date chips and selling to those wary of computers.

But it is extremely difficult to extrapolate from current patterns of use. Hardware and software are bound to be changed dramatically as data processing, storage and communications power increases and costs fall. Perhaps very powerful computers will be used as multi-purpose devices, or current product groups will become more rigid. Or perhaps this is too conservative, and a huge variety of different home computers will proliferate: music machines, database access machines (CD-I?), word processors, etc. The home computer of today is typically a stand-alone device, and is recognisably a machine that is employed for a limited number of data-processing tasks. It is quite possible that future home computers may be relatively 'invisible'. Not only will dedicated computers be built into appliances, but a device that is largely a computer may be thought of in other terms—say, as a communications device, a notepad, even as a companion. Instead of being sold a technology (the computer) looking for a use (games? solving your business problems?), consumers may be sold a specific service or set of services (entertainment, communications, energy management, security, etc.). Furthermore, although this is only just becoming evident, computers' communications and data storage capacities may well be increasingly prominent. Let us take this point further.

There have been several obstacles to the diffusion of home computers, which must have contributed to the small market in some countries, and the largely young, male-dominated pattern of use in other cases (Table 5.4). But a perhaps fundamental problem is that, for applications to domestic tasks, home computers need to be able to utilise information on real events, not just the rules of computer games. To access data, home computers require either:

— laborious typing-in of records concerning household accounts or similar data;
— linkages to other domestic equipment that can provide data—but at present the technology for achieving this is still immature, often expensive, and largely unfamiliar;
— access to information sources supplied online via viewdata or from online databases of some sort (perhaps even broadcast sources such as teletext);
— or access to information sources provided via stored data in CD systems, or the like—but, as with online sources, the production of such material for domestic users is at very early stages.

Many of the obstacles cited in Table 5.4 are being overcome, in the course of developments largely aimed at work-related and hobbyist users. Thus, computers targeted equally at small businesses and home users are now incorporating considerable processing power, floppy (and sometimes Winchester) discs, and sophisticated, user-friendly WIMP-type programming environments are now standard features of some machines costing less than £400. These are often 'packaged' with keyboard, VDU, disc drives, 'mice', and even printers and other peripherals being sold together as the basic unit (rather like rack hi-fi systems). Maintenance and even training services are provided on an uneven basis, but many retailers are now making these available.

What remains outstanding, however, is the input of useful data (other than those that have to be user-input—text, numbers for home accounts, details of the stamp collection, etc.). Developments in data storage (e.g. CD-I) and communications systems (e.g. viewdata) which should overcome these obstacles are rapidly unfolding; but whether the products that result will be thought of as home computers is questionable.

Several empirical studies of the dominant patterns of home computer use that have developed to date suggest that there are several main patterns of use. Perhaps we should first acknowledge the ex-users: an unknown proportion of consumers, perhaps often impulse buyers tempted by bargain offers of very cheap devices—fairly sophisticated first-generation home computers were retailed in the United Kingdom for as little as £30 during the home computer shake-out—have simply abandoned the use of their machines.

Table 5.4   Factors limiting the market for home computers

- *Non-user-friendly software and equipment.* This has meant that some familiarity with programming is often required even in order to get, say, a word processing or games programme to run. It has deterred many unfamiliar with IT from exploring home computers.
- *Inconvenient and inadequate input and output systems.* Data and programmes may take many minutes to load from a tape recorder, while other storage media (e.g. disc drives) have been relatively expensive. Display on TV screens and cheap VDUs is often of poor quality. Some keyboards have been too small and poorly designed for serious text input. All of these factors restrict serious use.
- *Unreliable hardware and poorly serviced software.* The early Sinclair machines were notable, but not alone, in achieving an unsavoury reputation for malfunctions and late delivery.
- *Lack of forward or reverse compatibility.* Sometimes this has been such that even a minor upgrade to a home computer means that one's software will not run on it, while new cables and plugs are necessary for peripherals. This has limited the volume of software available, and reduced incentives to improve equipment (e.g. with memory upgrades) to make it more versatile.
- *'Non-transparent' costs.* Prospective users are uncertain of how much additional hardware and software they will need to purchase, how expensive telecommunications services will prove in practice, etc.

Presvelou (1986a) reports four patterns of home computer use in Dutch households: similar pictures appear to emerge in other countries. In order of importance these are:

- computer hobbyism: rather than any specific intrinsic goal, the consumer is fascinated by exploring computer hardware and software;
- leisure activities: games, applications to hobbies (e.g. databases for collections or genealogy);
- household applications: a wide range of applications of programmes like spreadsheets/databases (financial management, inventories, compiling recipes), word processing (personal correspondence), educational software (for children's homework);
- and professional applications: word processing and access to online data services.[13]

In Britain, home computers were often bought as an educational device for children (or adults worried about being under-equipped to deal with the 'information society'). But, outstandingly, the main application is for playing computer games, and this is the main attraction for many young users (whatever they persuaded their parents about educational benefits). Some commentators seem to regard this as evidence for the ultimate insignificance of HI, apparently on the grounds that games are not 'serious' activities, or, even worse, that they are pandering to the worst human attributes. Sceptics refer to this in their critique of the social attitudes and political ideas conveyed and reinforced by computer games involving war game situations or centring on the 'zapping' of aliens (or worse: some games involve sexual violence). This critique is not unjustified, and it does highlight, in a negative way, the fact that leisure activities can be socially significant. (It also draws attention to the adolescent male mentality of many games enthusiasts.)

More positively, HI leisure activities can familiarise people with the use and limitations of technologies, and they can stimulate curiousity in how the systems work. Not all games are violent: some are humorous, some pose intellectual puzzles, some test reflexes or even general knowledge. Some psychologists argue that computer games encourage children to learn to construct mental models and learn systems of rules.[14]

If a major use of home computers is for games, many other applications also involve exploratory play. For example, hobbyists' devotion to finding out how their machines work, and to persuading them to fulfil certain objectives—one author announced that he was to publish *How to Make Your Micro Sit Up and Beg*, and another published *The Secret Guide to Computers*— is self-educative, often constructive, but often primarily ludic activity. (It also seems to contain a strong element of the masculine effort to master nature and machinery, to 'get inside' things and get them to submit: see Easlea (1984) for non-IT examples of this.) The 'household applications' identified by Presvelou are also often hobby-related—indeed, putting a database of one's home finance or collections onto a home computer has to be a labour of love! Formal work-related activities are also important applications of home computers, and even these have elements of play in them—the professional struggling to produce her/his own graphics and Desk Top publications. Household application and semi-professional applications are liable to remain and perhaps grow in significance, but hobbyism may well decline (at least relatively) as systems become more user-friendly, less 'exotic' and mysterious.

Home computers form an interesting case of movement towards HI. They represent a new consumer product that was not anticipated by most market analysts and computer specialists. It was very much pioneered by new small firms from the IT sector. The usual consumer electronics firms have made few inroads here, although Amstrad have successfully capitalised on the maturation of technologies and the potential for large markets for standardised equipment. For educational, entertainment and professional applications, the market for home computers has been established. However, it remains to be seen whether the future development of this market will be self-contained, whether home computers will tend to merge with CD-I or similar devices, or become part of a more general shift towards home automation (discussed in Chapter 6).

5.8 Concluding Notes

One theme running throughout both this and the preceding chapter has been the significance of *standards* in HI and related fields. With increased prominence being given to technical standards, it may well be time to review the appropriateness of international standard-setting bodies to cope with the proliferation of new media and services.

A second theme concerns the evolution of consumer demand for radically new products. Our account suggests that some lessons seem to have been learned by many, but not all, industrialists and policymakers. Most significant, perhaps, is the shift away from marketing *technologies* to marketing *services*, a transition that has been easier for some sectors and firms to make than for others. (Very broadly, it seems that consumer electronics and broadcasting companies have adapated better than mainframe computer and telecommunications companies.) The role of 'trigger services' in establishing footholds for new systems has been widely recognised.

The trigger services prioritised vary according to national economic and political contexts. Without political intervention—and in some cases, in line with political ideologies—entertainment is often the main trigger forming a focus of industrial activity. But welfare-related triggers are also the focus of some interest, as is apparent in the agenda of the Sotech programme, in discussions in the European Community around IRIS (Initiative for Research in Social Applications of Informatics), and in the many efforts to develop viewdata and teletext services for disabled and housebound people.

Education, too, may act as a significant trigger. Much of the innovation here will take place within the formal educational system, and thus have relevance to HI only indirectly (for example, if the Domesday Project leads to the reduction of videodisc costs and familiarises potential users of HI). But some innovations—for example in distance learning through computer communication systems—could prove significant in the diffusion of facilities to households.[15]

Thus, policy measures in public services are liable to be significant influences on the development of HI. In the absence of proactive public service innovations, it is likely that some private service equivalents will develop—for example, in home security and health care. And some utilities have an interest in HI, as we shall see in the next chapter. But entertainment and certain forms of social interaction (e.g. the *messagerie* in Teletel) are liable to remain the main driving forces for HI in the absence of such initiatives.

A final, related, point concerns the tension between strategies of HI innovation based on an evolutionary upgrading of existing goods and services, and that based on more revolutionary change requiring the transformation of whole systems. We have encountered this in several instances—ISDN, HDTV and CD-V and in the next chapter IHS will provide us with yet another case. There are few general rules that can provide guidance here (see Chapter 3), but two points need to be made. First, the nature of the product and consumer market are significant (how far is the product stand-alone? How frequently are the relevant durables renewed? Is there synergy with a business market?). Second, this is again an issue where the role of public authority action—in setting standards, procuring equipment, providing complementary services—may well be critical to the technological trajectory that emerges . . . and to its social implications.

Notes

1. See, for example, Rothschild (1984) on the 'auto-industrial age'.
2. The terms 'brown goods' and 'white goods' derive from the typical colour of the first products to widely diffuse as consumer electronics and motorised kitchen appliances. The terms suggest the importance of innovations in the chemicals and metalworking industries that made possible, for example, low-cost bakelite and lightweight white-enamelled metal goods. For practical reasons, motor cars are rarely white—a colour particularly well-suited to efforts to establish images of kitchens (and electric power itself) as clean and hygenic.
3. See Gershuny (1977).
4. Cawson *et al.* (1986) use the term 'passive protectionism', in an interesting discussion of government policymaking in this field.
5. Reported by Spinks (1985).
6. The newsletter *CD-I News* published by LINK resources has covered the debates over technical standards for CD-ROM and CD-I. *CD-ROM* magazine has also begun to feature this discussion.
7. Fox (1987a); see also April and June 1987 issues of *CD-I News*.
8. Raun and Thomas (1987).
9. See Turner (1986a).
10. Valery (1977).
11. Schofield (1987b); this author estimates that of over two hundred micro-computers (including business machines) on sale in Britain in 1983, only around five survived to 1987; 90 per cent of machines had been discontinued, and a large proportion of the manufacturers had withdrawn from the microcomputer sector (or gone bankrupt).
12. Rapoport (1986).
13. Presvelou (1986a,b). On the use of home computers for playing games, see Murdock *et al.* (1985); Forester (1987) cites studies from the United States documenting games as the major use of home computers. Again I draw on the unpublished work of Leslie Haddon (1987) for points about 'computer culture'.
14. Sinha (1987): this report is based on papers and discussions at a meeting at Aarhus University, Denmark. For interesting case study material, see Turkle (1985). Surprisingly, with the exception of the Underwoods' chapter on education, a recent collection of psychological studies of IT (Blackler and Oborne, 1987) fails to address such points.
15. At the Home Informatics Workshop in London in November 1986, Maurer (1986) made an extremely interesting presentation and demonstration of a viewdata-delivered Computer-Aided Instruction system, which provides educational software to be downloaded for offline use. Mainly used by teachers in Germanic countries so far, and most extensively developed for topics like computer science and mathematics, this network is being used in an increasing number of countries, and offering material for languages, humanities, and even sports. The demonstration featured the Costoc database, which now contains

hundreds of CAI lessons in computer science, mainly in English language, with the chief aim being to provide material for tricky parts of lessons and projects. The system uses public viewdata networks and intelligent viewdata terminals (e.g. the Austrian MUPID terminal).

Another development here is a course on Information Technology being developed by the Open University in Britain. Students on this course will use home computers, linked to Open University databases and bulletin boards, to carry out assignments and research, submit essays, and interact with tutors. Finnegan *et al.* (1987) is a course reader for this series.

6 Towards the home of the future

6.1 Interactivity

This chapter presents perspectives on the future development of HI. This will be based on the discussions of previous chapters concerning technological trends, supplier strategies, and consumer uptake of new goods and services. We have already discussed developments in telecommunications and consumer electronics, both from a technological standpoint and in the light of what little research exists already concerning consumer use of new technologies. Now we will move on to consider some areas of application of IT within the home which have only been touched upon in passing so far. An underlying theme of this chapter is our effort to identify more precisely the specific contributions that IT may make to consumer goods and services.

To spell out this theme, it is the *interactive capabilities* of IT that will be of most importance to IT. What is this 'interactivity'? Essentially, it is the capacity of IT-based systems to deliver responses—often complex and continuously changing responses—to changing inputs. The interactivity may be with:

— other devices (for example, signals sent from 'white goods' to a home computer or peritelevision system);
— physical environments (for example, sensors detecting changes in temperature levels or airborne pollutants);
— telecommunications systems (for example, data inputs from information services like Radio Data Services or from remote users or people trying to get in touch with householders);
— users (for example, householders or visitors supplying inputs directly through keyboard or voice commands).

IT systems behave in a programmed way, although their programming can often be changed by users; but their interactive capabilities mean that they need not always behave according to one fixed sequence of responses. In effect, they are goal-directed: they are programmed to achieve particular effects in changing circumstances.

These capabilities allow for users to interact with HI systems so as to gain access to appropriate data and knowledge, and to have these and other outputs 'tailored' to personal requirements. They also allow for HI systems to interact with environments: to control home equipment according to data on changing immediate physical or social circumstances, or to messages delivered via telecommunications that announce such changes ('rain is expected', 'I'll be home at eight'). This interactivity will be a key feature of those innovations in HI that go beyond simple improvements to existing products. It widens the scope for applying IT in both planning and decisionmaking activities in the home, and in controlling domestic circumstances.

This has important implications for the development of HI. In particular, it suggests that entertainment-type applications may become more interactive: the video game and the camcorder are examples of applications where the user's interaction with the technology is far more important in shaping the product than in 'passive entertainment' goods like TV and radio.[1] In terms of familiar white goods (and the automobile), interactivity may mean an augmentation of both planning and execution of tasks, with some additional information outputs to users, and some automation of tasks previously requiring human control. And the capability of applying technology to achieve results where direct human interaction has traditionally been required may lead to HI being applied to areas of activity where to date there has been little use of consumer technology: to transactions, and to what are mainly provided as collective services (health, education, etc.). But we shall begin with applications that are generally regarded as more frivolous—those in toys, games and sports.

6.2 Entertainment and leisure: playing with HI

We have already devoted considerable space to developments in audio and video entertainment systems, and to such topics as online computer games. But these are far from exhausting the range of entertainment products. Other types of games, toys and sports equipment are cases in point.

As in the case of home computers (discussed in Chapter 5), there is lively technology transfer between the *toy and game products* developed for consumer markets and the emerging professional applications of IT in formal work and other activities. For example, educational software is a source of inspiration for some intellectual games (mostly of the general knowledge and memorisation sort rather than puzzles), and computer games are an important influence on the design of educational software—and on professional simulations and applications of all sorts. Again, there are relations between the new products being developed here and other areas of HI. For example, hobbyists, developing control systems for their interests with model railways and similar devices, are leading the way for the control of other types of domestic equipment.

Several developments are already visible in the application of IT to toys and games (including those video games played by means of general-purpose home computers)—see Table 6.1. It is hardly surprising that the interactivity offered by the versatile new technology should be applied enthusiastically to

Table 6.1   Developments in toys and games

● More realistic simulations and effects during play (e.g. better computer graphics and sound effects, and the mimicking of real-life controls and displays on toys or junior versions of adult devices (e.g. 'computer bikes' with speedometers, sirens, etc.).

● Simple robotics, and more sophisticated radio/remote control of (and feedback from) motorised devices.

● More sophisticated adventure games, and games combining adventure game and graphic/arcade formats, with some convergence between these 'games' and cultural media (thus some software publishers and authors describe their games as 'interactive fiction'[2]).

● Computer versions of traditional games (e.g. chess, bridge, scrabble), reducing dependence on other human players and making it possible to play while travelling.

● And, in contrast, opportunities to play 'telegames', either traditional games mediated by computer-communications equipment with one other, or new multi-user games, as outlined earlier; while these games are currently somewhat restricted in terms of graphics and moving imagery, future developments will no doubt allow for more realistic visualisation of oneself and other players in these fantasy worlds (as is already the case in some arcade games which use videodiscs).

games and entertainment—especially in activities where some aroma of mystery and magic is sought. Magnetic and electrical games ('magic robot' puzzles, etc.) have been available for decades, and cheap recorders and now elementary speech synthesis have been used to lend more realism to dolls and other toys.

Talking dolls look set to become as much of a menace to those travelling by public transport as personal stereos. They make remarks in response to environmental change ('it's dark', 'where are we going?', etc.) and emit demands 'I'm hungry', 'I'm sleepy', etc.), with synchronised eye and mouth movements. Singing dolls are another hazard, on which we shall dwell no further. It should be noted that some critics argue that these remove the stimulus to children's imagination provided by traditional toys. This is an interesting criticism since the implication that interactive technology may diminish other kinds of interaction (with other people, or with mental constructs, as in imaginative play) is one that is echoed in other areas of HI.

The quest for greater realism is also manifest in video games, where more sophisticated consoles and computers are able to give remarkable graphic displays and sound effects. Domestic technology will probably continue to experience technology transfer from arcades; computer games have long attempted to emulate the qualities of arcade games on dedicated machines.

Arcade technology is now quite remarkable, with laser discs combining with computer graphics to provide movie-quality visual effects—with interactivity (and deafening stereo sound).[3] Simulators in the style of aircraft cockpits and motorcycles provide added realism, with seats that tilt and shake. In Japan, videodisc technology—but not as yet simulator equipment —has been marketed to consumers for games purposes, and CD-I is seen as a plausible future extension. And in the United States, Mattel Toys plan an interactive CD version of their ominously titled children's TV series *Captain Power and the Soldiers of the Future*.[4]

This TV series is itself described as 'interactive' since it allows for the viewer to score points by shooting at characters on the screen with a special toy gun.[5] This delightful innovation can be seen as part of a more general tendency for toy and TV/movie producers to coordinate product marketing. This is apparent throughout the West, with 'spin-off' characters from films being prominent among toys and models; but an even more lucrative development in North America are the toys that are triggered into action by signals in the TV programmes in which they are featured. This gives the child deprived of the tie-in toys added evidence with which to wage the struggle for a larger collection with its parents.

A related type of electronic device applies IT to adult and juvenile *sport and exercise equipment*. Already luxury IT-based rowing and cycling machines, treadmills, etc., can be acquired for home exercise studios. These use microelectronics to provide records of and feedback on individual performance, to help set performance goals and training regimes, and to provide more realistic simulation of the real-life sport situation (e.g. one rowing machine displays a computer game-type video image of the position of one's canoe relative to 'competitors', and plays applause when one's performance is above standard).[6]

As with the arcade and the consumer video game, so we may expect to see transfer of innovations from the formal economy of health studios to private households' sports equipment—at least, to the larger and more affluent ones—and to community centres. An example of an exercise system introduced in some four hundred health clubs in the United States is 'Living Well Company's Powercise', whose European introduction is planned for late 1987. Each of a set of six exercise machines provides feedback on users' performance via voice synthesis (a vocabulary of a thousand words is possessed) and images representing a very basic human face on a VDU; various 'personalities' able to adopt simulated emotional states coach the user through activities. The devices intercommunicate so that their programmes can be adjusted in the light of the others' results, and they also communicate with a talking-scale and printer.[7]

6.3 'Pets' and 'comforters': technological society?

Computer communications seem to offer considerable prospects for greater social intercourse, at least for isolated individuals and groups in an impersonal urban society: consider the use of Teletel by the hard-of-hearing and insomniacs. But some commentators suggest that IT actually reinforces solitude—if not the reflective solitude of the ascetic. This is a common criticism made against computer games (and, presumably, it was levelled against books and TV in earlier periods—which is not to deny that it may have some force). The implication is that interactivity involving IT equipment is liable to displace social interaction: that involvement with IT media may be more exciting and/or less troubling that involvement with people.

Two developments that are currently regarded as frivolities of little significance may be of some importance in this respect. First is the 'petster'—a robotic toy being promoted by one of the founders of Apple computers, that can perform a variety of simple functions. The version that is modelled on the cat, for example, can 'explore' a room (its learning capacity is currently very restricted), approach someone at the sound of a handclap, emit purring and other noises. The inventors claim that the petster is preferable to a real animal in that it requires no feeding, cleaning-up, or furniture repair; how serious they are about this is doubtful, but it is worth considering the advertising blurb with which this gadget is being promoted in the United Kingdom: 'Your new electronic pet obeys your voice commands, will respond at the clap of your hands and saves a fortune in vet's bills. Open the door and he wakes up. Ignore him and he'll go to sleep, so is a real pet this agreeable?'[8] There are still some advantages to living organisms, of course: the petster cannot chase and catch mice. But its novelty value might be enhanced by the innovation of robotic mice—'peststers'?—which would provide lively entertainment as competing robots war it out on the living room carpet.

While the petster is little more than an expensive conversation-piece, it does suggest directions for the future development of robotic toys—and these are generally more readily achievable than the applications of robotics to useful purpose in the home.[9] Even the 'robot waiters' that are currently available (e.g. the 'Omnibot', advertised as an 'electronic butler') really do little more than the petster. The limit of their ability is following routes, playing cassette tapes, and carrying drinks and peanuts (or, in more sophisticated models, actually mixing the drinks, with little more robotic technology than the average food processor). One version of the petster provides a more 'interactive' audio output: it stimulates conversational abilities, by uttering a garbled form of the last words (and voice tones) that it has experienced: this seems to appeal to children, who are able to attribute meaning to the 'reply' and conduct conversations. While stimulating childish imaginations, this may do little for children's ability to engage in real conversations, where attention to what other people actually say may be rather more important.

The second development is that of computer programmes that simulate conversational and counselling functions: we might call these comforters. The Californian term for these is 'psycheware'.[10] As well as the well-known versions of the 'psychotherapeutic' programme Eliza—according to some accounts originally written as a joke—there are numerous programmes that offer personality tests, provide advice on childcare problems, engage in astrological or bio-rhythm analysis, or even simulate particular stereotypical relatives. The sophistication and seriousness of such programmes varies dramatically, as might be expected.[11] There are numerous anecdotal reports that suggest that some individuals become engaged with such psycheware in the same kind of way that others become video game addicts or dedicated hackers.

A small fraction of the population will probably always find some fantasy activity in which to work out (or work deeper into) psychic stresses. IT's interactivity creates new opportunities here, but many methods are familiar: drugs, encounter groups, high-risk sports, meditation, dance and drama therapy, and many more. Nevertheless, the two IT applications described immediately above do suggest that technological innovation might be leading to devices that would appeal to wider groups. For example, many lonely or insecure people find solace in pets: will improved petsters and psycheware prove even more capable of meeting/feeding their needs? This seems to be regarded as a positive development, at least judging by the way in which we have been urged to invest in fifth-generation research in order to, *inter alia*, be able to create 'computer companions' for elderly people . . . friends who will never tire of hearing one's reminiscences, [12] or, perhaps, little companions who will boost one's ego by providing a continuous stream of flattery?

We can only fantasise about—or use good science fiction[13] to gain insight into—the devices that will be realised in the wake of the innovations stimulated by the 'fifth generation' research programmes of various countries; for these efforts should eventually deliver computing power capable of the extremely complex task of speech recognition and natural language processing at relatively low prices. But existing markets for toys and pets (and TV sets) do appear to be in part based on keeping children or elderly and other lonely people safely occupied; and extensions of such markets using even quite primitive forms of HI are not impossible.

The problem with such a development is that it may not merely alleviate the symptoms of privatism and social isolation. It can also accentuate the underlying problems, by rendering people less skilled in relating to each others' experiences (including difficult, conflictual, or unpleasant ones), and less mindful of the value of doing so. Such problems need to be attended to *before* such devices are rendered acceptable by purely commercial pressures. Already there are signs that in some circumstances people will prefer machine to human interactions: for instance, although we should be mindful of the specific circumstances of the case, experiments in Britain with a computer-based system to aid unemployed people search for job vacancies have shown that this is generally preferred to the traditional means of interacting with an employment official. The prospect arises of generations whose abilities to engage in meaningful discourse, and to tolerate (and learn and grow from) the (necessary rather than the merely superfluous) frustrations of dealing with real people will be seriously eroded.

6.4 Home security systems

A relatively new development in household goods is the transfer of techno-logies of alarm and security, initially created in military, industrial and medical settings, to many homes. Some of these technologies have previously been applied by affluent households with many possessions to guard, but some of the systems are quite novel, and the degree of diffusion is much wider than heretofore. Many stand-alone alarm systems have appeared on the market. These roughly fall into three main classes.

First come detectors of smoke, fire and other untoward environmental conditions. Here security devices merge with devices designed for less urgent conditions, such as detectors of domestic atmospheric pollution, which are intended to operate ventilation systems rather than to set off alarms.

Second come detectors of intruder presence—of motion, body heat, or tampering with doors, windows or household devices. (For example, it is possible to buy a cassette-sized alarm that fits into a VTR and warns if it is being moved.)

Third come emergency buttons and alarms that can be activated by (in particular) elderly and disabled people who find themselves in trouble. As well as fixed systems, these include buttons worn on the body so that they can be activated in the event of the user being immobilised by a fall out of reach of a telephone.

The first two of these classes of alarm system parallel those technological developments in 'white goods' that add safety features to familiar household devices, and that allow for their operation via proximity detectors or telecommunications. The third class resembles those developments that allow for remote control of household equipment.

The diffusion of such devices is facilitated both by substantial market changes (e.g. the growth of elderly, single-person households, fears of burglary and increasing value of private property in the average household, and changes in local authority social service and policing provisions); and by technological developments that have made available, at relatively low cost devices that are efficient (the cost of 'crying wolf' and mistakenly calling out emergency services can be very high, as can the cost of silence when real problems are present) and that are fairly secure against unauthorised tampering.

Technological innovation is rapid here. Among the most important of the emerging innovations are those designed to network such alarms so that any device may set off, as appropriate, one or several responses to a problem. These responses may include audio devices (bells, klaxons), visual devices (warning lights, floodlights, messages on screens), even automated telephone calls using voice synthesis. An interesting indication of the sorts of actors that may promote such developments is the 'Telecom Security' system currently on offer from British Telecom. This offers door sensors, interior movement sensors, heat and smoke sensors, and emergency buttons—and these are connected to warning sirens and, through the telephone operator, to emergency services.

Another development is that towards more unobtrusive systems, which are designed so as not to make a bad situation worse by alarming the wrong people. But security devices are often used as deterrents to warn off intruders. Thus there is a market in dummy alarms which are positioned visibly outside houses. Devices that simulate occupation by turning lights on and off randomly, or set off sound effects (barking dogs are a favourite) when the doorbell is rung represent a further line of development.

Security devices may diffuse as private consumer goods, as is currently very prevalent (attested, for example, by advertisements in popular magazines, and the prominence of such equipment in DIY shops and locksmiths). But they may also be the focus of policy interventions, especially welfare initiatives.

Many local authorities have taken steps in this direction, and while this is often taken as a self-contained measure, in other cases there is a longer-term strategic vision (on the part of public authorities and/or equipment suppliers) supportive of broader developments in the direction of home automation. For example, Honeywell has recently entered into a £400,000 contract with a British local authority (South Tyneside) to provide a system linking two thousand sheltered homes to the town hall; eventually ten times this number of homes will be networked. This is seen as part of a major 'smart building' project, also involving libraries and hospitals, and providing fire alarms and energy and building management facilities. In the first instance, local minicomputers will communicate alarm messages to the town hall mainframe, which will alert wardens and provide them with such data as the name of the relevant doctor.[14] Police authorities may also see merit in initiating or building upon such developments: following a period where police strategies have moved away from traditional 'community' policing, there is growing effort to involve neighbourhoods and other state agencies in crime prevention, and there is evidence of some interest in relating these revised strategies to technological developments in the home.

Clearly, while demographic change is an important vector of these developments, they are also fed by increasing social isolation and by 'urban paranoia'. Perhaps the home will become more of a fortress, if such trends continue; perhaps there will be more effort towards establishing guarded enclaves for the affluent, or urban planning to establish 'defensible space' (or even to reverse the social isolation that has been effectively designed into the physical structure of many communities). If the home does become a fortress, the doors and windows may acquire characteristics of hi-tech drawbridges and portcullises! Video systems to monitor (and record) callers may replace eyeholes and audio systems (such audio systems are already common in apartment buildings, and video systems are beginning to appear here). Electronic door locks may be operated by personal laser cards (or eventually voice or palmprint recognition?) or provide information on the use of keys, and be linked to alarm and other home automation systems.

6.5 'White' goods: HI for housework?

We have seen that the early applications of electronics to 'white goods' were mainly to their controls and displays. This is because the core functions of white goods usually involve effecting physical or physico-chemical transformations based on motor power and combustion, and thus IT is mainly appropriate for managing and reporting on these operations.

Microelectronics and related technologies are now used extensively in these applications, for example in touch panel controls and screen displays. Furthermore, IT is also being applied to a number of informational tasks that have previously relied upon the perception and decisionmaking of the user. This is perhaps particularly evident in the new cooking technology of microwave devices, where recent models of microwave oven are equipped with sensors and probes to weigh the food, measure the vapours emitted, and assess its temperature. Similar features can be introduced into conventional ovens. Another important development is that cookers are becoming programmable, so that a large number of different sets of cooking instructions can be stored and acted upon; standard cooking routines can be provided, or users can enter their own requirements (adapted, say, to family size). Safety features are also important; thus one of the items described at the Home Informatics workshop as developed within the United States 'smart house' framework (about which more in Section 6.7 below) is a stove that cannot be switched on by a child since it only works when proximity detectors are activated by the presence of someone of adult height.

Features like these are not, of course, restricted to cookers: they are, indeed, likely to be standard in white goods in the future. Thus, washing machines with touch-panel controls can offer standard programmes—future generations of such equipment may be able to act upon (and probably learn) user instructions for unusual requirements—and the associated drying machines will adapt speed of operation, heat and air flow according to measurements of load weight, moisture and temperature, or to specific instructions (designed, for example, to shrink jeans).

While large and expensive devices are particularly liable to see such IT innovations, small displays and safety-featured touch controls can also be built into many portable tools, for example. Innovations in the construction industry like ultrasonic 'tape measures' are liable to diffuse to the home. Even devices like taps and light switches can be operated by proximity detectors (e.g. infra-red systems that respond to the presence of a hand), while power points can be made safe even for little fingers, as we shall see later.

New functions are also being developed in white goods. Examples include the now familiar multi-purpose food processor, and simple Computer Aided Design-type systems that are incorporated in to advanced sewing and knitting machines, and that may in the future be added to DIY power tools. Such equipment will feature improved displays which indicate their status (operation complete, power supply interrupted, food about to burn), and provide diagnostic information if there seem to be faults. Again, even small devices may also feature such new functions: there has been, for example, attention to the redesign of such a basic item as the tape measure, for instance by providing not only digital displays but also calculator functions (e.g. ability to store measurements and calculate areas and angles). The most significant new functions for white goods are likely to involve communications, which will be taken up further below, when we consider home automation.

Before leaving the discussion of HI applied to areas of informal, domestic work activity, we should note two further areas of application, both of which have been touch on in preceding chapters. First is the automobile, which has already proved to be a consumer good ripe for the application of microelectronics (if not strictly a 'white good'). As well as the systems that use voice synthesis to warn drivers of engine problems (or infringement of speed limits or seatbelt regulations), IT is used to improve the operating efficiency of motor cars. Several innovations discussed earlier are already being oriented towards drivers—mobile communications (cellular phones and text-display systems), especially for business users, and CD-I for route-planning. Assistance with automobile maintenance and trouble-shooting is already provided on floppy disc for some classes of car owner (and interactive videodisc for engineers and dealers): it is easy to imagine such aids being linked via home computers to diagnostics output from informatised engine, brake and other car systems.

A second type of informal work that is not (at present) carried out extensively from within the home is shopping, and the activities around it. Two areas of innovation are apparent, although each is often viewed with scepticism: household stock management, and teleshopping. The first of these can be dealt with quickly: while home computers are in some ways ideally suited to keeping records of consumption and goods held in stock—

Table 6.2   Factors which may facilitate teleshopping systems

● Teleshopping's current utility is restricted because of the inadequate visual information provided on products; improved telecommunications systems, or combinations of data storage and communications, are liable to change this.

● Teleshopping systems have been handicapped in offering a wide range or large number of items by the cumbersome procedures of moving through menu layers and the like associated with viewdata and similar frameworks: improved software and HMIs are liable to change this, perhaps rendering an experience simulating conventional shopping.

● Mail order and telephone shopping are becoming very popular, and the computer systems set up to cope with such activities can often be applied to teleshopping (this is the case, for example, for the system operated by one US company that uses telephone advertising and telephone keypresses as its new mode of access to remote customers; a similar TV shopping system has been launched in Europe on satellite TV).

● IT itself cannot deliver the goods ordered by teleshoppers. Among other consequences this means that delivery innovations are required. As teleshopping diffuses—perhaps for high-value goods at first—such innovations (with scale economies) are more feasible. Possibilities include flexible delivery times and schedules, neighbourhood deposit centres (e.g. post offices), and household deposit centres (refrigerated post boxes, new types of door).

● Electronic Funds Transfer systems of various kinds are being introduced, and these facilitate the use of telecommunications for transactional purposes.

and thus for planning family budgets and shopping lists—a major problem is confronted. How is the information to be input to the computer? The hobbyists who have attempted to apply HI to these purposes have usually tired rapidly of the amount of keyboarding necessary to keep up to date.

A technical 'fix' to this problem may be on the horizon, however. An increasing proportion of the goods that are purchased are bar-coded (as part of innovation within the retail sector). Why not equip the refrigerator and storage cupboards with bar-code readers which could then be used to keep a record of items added to and taken from household storage areas? With appropriate linkages to computer facilities, and the use of 'smart' software that could estimate how frequently certain items need to be acquired (and thus issue reminders to shoppers), and printers that could even prepare a first draft shopping list, a really useful facility could be introduced. One drawback of such a system is that it would be vulnerable to disruption by midnight munchers who forgot to use the bar-code reader, and children who are keen to increase the order for favourite foodstuffs!

As for teleshopping, we have already noted the limited success of the experiments that have been carried out to date. In the long term, however, teleshopping via computer-communications is liable to be of substantial importance. A number of reasons for this are cited in Table 6.2.

Shopping and other transactional activities (e.g. banking) are ones where the interactive capabilities of HI make innovation likely. We shall now turn to other areas where interactivity plays a central role—personal care and 'home automation'.

6.6 Personal care goods: HI for healthy living?

Care of the body and the provision of comfort would seem to be activities that are particularly resistant to IT innovation. Even so, the incorporation of audio and even video entertainment facilities into the bathroom and bedroom is not uncommon, and devices like hairdryers and even baths (e.g. jacuzzis and whirlpool baths) and wardrobes have been the focus of some gimmicky microelectronics applications.

Much personal care requires physical attention to bodily needs, and given that the immediate prospects for much development of home robotics are rather limited, HI is unlikely to play a major role here. Control of lifting and moving equipment in the home to ease the life of elderly and disabled people is certainly not unthinkable, but this is likely to be considerably less than (highly expensive) true robotics, where the device is able to be programmed to undertake various complex sequences of movement. Equipment to make beds and change clothes is far away from most needy homes, while elaborate motorised wheelchairs and communications systems for paraplegics are already in evidence. What we can expect to see is the application of simple (and relatively cheap) IT controls and mechanical power to basic and repetitive physical tasks (opening and closing doors and windows, moving dustbins, etc.).

But HI may still find wide applications to personal care, for many aspects of health maintenance and everyday care routines involve information-processing as well as physical and biological processes. It is probable that some of the more health-oriented aspects of personal care, which require informational inputs as well as, if not more than, material ones, will be the focus of HI innovation and of the diffusion of equipment from the formal economy (medical services in particular) into the household.

One class of such innovations follows on from the alarms discussed above. *Baby alarms* of various sorts have diffused widely in recent years: one popular model simply plugs into an electric power point, and uses mains signalling to alert people in one room if noises are being made in another. (This is marketed as a home security device as well as a baby alarm.) More sophisticated devices that can monitor the breathing or physiological status of infants believed to be prone to 'cot death' (Sudden Infant Mortality

Syndrome) and other health emergencies (in vulnerable adults as well as children, of course) are available.

Similar monitoring equipment is also likely to emerge for applications such as unobtrusively monitoring elderly or handicapped relatives (a further technological extension of current alarm buttons, of external lights asking for help that can be activated within the home, and of the low-tech, more informal and traditional systems where friends or neighbours take note of whether milk bottles are being put out or newspapers collected). It has even been proposed that authorities should be in a position to be sure that at least one room in an elderly person's house in meeting minimum temperature standards in wintertime—and an experiment using mains signalling for this purpose is under way in the United Kingdom.[15]

Health monitoring systems form a second, increasingly related, area of innovation. Such systems have been traditionally developed for people with chronic health problems (e.g. diabetes and heart disorder).[16] But many single items of equipment, and more sophisticated systems, are now being produced. Some are aimed at the general population, others at trigger groups such as sports enthusiasts and the parents of small children. Thus, one stream of innovation is closely associated with the developments in sports equipment, and the associated concern with healthy living, which has been discussed above. And one stream of innovation is associated with childcare.

Many minor items of medical/health equipment are the focus of IT innovation. Digital thermometers (which are also advertised so as to appeal to parents), pulse meters and sphygamometers are being retailed to consumers as more accurate and easy to use than traditional equipment. Significantly, such devices may be applied not only routinely, but also in conjunction with exercise programmes. In the latter case, the data may be correlated with performance data, in order to assess exercise regimes that will improve physical fitness without imposing too much stress. (Recall the sports studio equipment discussed previously.) At present the user typically has to note data from one device and enter them into another (a home computer for example); however, it is no great step to intercommunicating devices.

A third stream of innovation is associated with biofeedback, where there has been interest from several quarters (including 'alternative therapists') in helping individuals learn how to relax, or to attain meditative states, by skin resistance or brain wave monitoring. Equipment to enable home computer owners to achieve such monitoring is readily available: for example, Synapse Software market a floppy disc for Atari and Commodore home computers which is used in conjunction with biofeedback equipment to provide oscilloscope readings (the user is given goals to aim at in changing these readings), and also features computer graphics and game-like activities designed to promote relaxation. (Here a convergence of psycheware and sports/health HI seems to be developing).[17] Other medical applications may also find consumer markets: for example, biofeedback techniques have been developed to improve posture (by giving feedback on changes in one's back positions) and physical performance. And more versatile equipment is being developed, such as the Japanese 'intelligent toilet' which analyses heart rate, blood pressure, temperature, urine content, and the like (and which can transmit the data by telephone to one's doctor).[18]

Such innovations might actually be fostered by (public or private) medical services, where they could be used to improve the formal services' analysis of individual health. (As well as enabling better service outputs, this could increase the efficiency and profitability of private medical insurance schemes). Greater self-service monitoring—for example, clients undertaking chemical tests on their own blood or urine samples (as in some pregnancy tests and blood sugar analysers today)—is one possibility that would enable reductions in the labour inputs by medical and paramedical practitioners, and save on time clients' needs to spend in formal medical institutions. A further step involves remote monitoring of clients with medical staff relating to the clients via telecommunications and basic health monitoring equipment used at home. Trial studies suggest that this could save a considerable proportion of costs involved in treating some chronic disorders which require very regular treatment and monitoring.

Development of such systems may accordingly be mainly stimulated by the formal medical services themselves. Alternatively, they may emerge later in consequence of growing consumer interest in, say, health-oriented CD-I and computer programmes, which substitute for traditional family health encyclopaedias and allow for more self-diagnosis and reorientation of lifestyle. Perhaps one will be able to choose between a variety of alternative medical philosophies as expert systems come on disc.

Such innovations could well blend into more general concerns with maximising the quality of one's life, for example by integrating diet, exercise, stress, psycheware and medical information systems together. If the latter innovation dynamic predominates, it may well be that major markets for health and personal care innovations will be created.

But these would then not so much be markets of the (relatively poor) elderly and infirm; rather they would mainly consist of the (more affluent) middle-class young and middle-class aged. They may cater to growing health-oriented demands, but not really meet the serious medical needs of the less healthy. It is quite likely that such an innovation pattern will be followed, since it appears to coincide both with concerns for healthy living and with critiques of Welfare State provisions. However, it is not necessarily the case that this pattern would prevent formal health services themselves seeking to improve service efficiency or effectiveness by diffusing IT equipment to households. We return to this topic in the next chapter, where we shall also consider the challenges that may be posed to other formal welfare services, such as education, by similar HI innovation dynamics.

6.7 HI to IHS: towards home automation?

The MSX specification for Japanese home computers (see Chapter 5) may not have ensured them success in Western markets, but it did alert the Western IT industry to the ability of Japanese manufacturers to standardise software (and communications) protocols. Japan-watchers pointed out that MSX was more than a standard for computer games; it was a basis for different computers to be equally able to control other items of consumer electronics. With the dominance of Japanese firms in many areas of consumer electronics, and the activity of these firms across a broad range of markets, it was perceived that new challenges might be confronted as the technical possibility of interconnecting items of domestic equipment grew. Matsushita, for example, have produced a rather tacky promotional video, aimed at raising awareness among American consumers of its 'smart house' system; if it achieves nothing else, this demonstrates the preparations being made to establish new markets here.

In the United States a 'smart house' project was launched as a multi-company initiative following a 1984 initiative by the National Association of Homebuilders.[19] This made use of the 1984 National Joint Ventures Act, which encourages firms to engage in joint R&D. (This Act was itself a response to Japanese R&D models.) Among the forty or so companies involved are computer firms (e.g. Apple, IBM) and telecommunications companies (e.g. AT&T, Bell-Northern), as well as companies involved in heating and ventilation, bathroom and kitchen appliances, consumer electronics, etc.

A focal activity of this project has been the development of new home wiring systems: current domestic wiring has been criticised as over-complicated and marginally safe, which, while requiring seven different electrical contractors for each home, fails to exploit its technical possibilities extensively and restricts innovation. Already the project has achieved change in the specifications of the US wiring code: so, for example, it becomes possible to integrate communications and power on the same wiring. (An example of this is the 'smart appliance', which, when required to operate, sends a signal down the wire to ask for the power supply to be turned on.) A smart house plug and socket system has been designed which carries power and analogue and digital communications lines, together with optional coaxial and fibre optic cable lines.

The US project's product interface specifications were availably by early 1986, and R&D contracts, funded by participants, were issued that summer. The 'smart house' group anticipates that smart house systems will be sold through their entertainment functions in the first instance, and demonstration systems are on tour. Original forecasts that some five thousand houses would be available in 1987 (just as show houses) have already proved to be underestimates, and projections are for hundreds of thousands of smart houses to be built per annum by 1990. It is important to note that there is a high rate of home construction in North America, and that the estimated costs of installing a smart house system are only some $500 additional to an average house price of $137,000.

European interest in home automation materialised at around the same time: a Eureka programme (costing £12 million to start up) was established in 1987 in what Europeans dubbed 'Interactive Home Systems' (IHS). (Recall that HDTV is another area of Eureka activity.) This programme involves such European firms as Philips, GEC, Thorn-EMI, Thomson, Siemens and Electrolux. (These account for large proportions of white and brown goods manufacture in Europe.) The stimulus for this initiative was British activities, organised around an 'IHS Task Force' set up in late 1984 by the National Economic Development Office's Consumer Electronics Economic Development Committee. Again, the impetus for its activities was the perceived Japanese challenge around new consumer electronics. In contrast to the US and Japanese approaches, the emphasis here so far is less on creating new markets, more on improving existing products. It has been more concerned with upgrading proven products (including those from different European manufacturers), so that they may be interconnected, than with the achievement of futuristic high technology that may run too far in advance of consumer interests.[20]

Standards are again an important part of this programme. The Europeans started out from the position that they need not necessarily accept American standards, and their core project centres on interconnection. It seeks to encourage separate manufacturers to create devices with standards enabling devices to work in a coordinated fashion—or at least to coexist without interference—across the various media available for in-home communications (e.g. mains signalling, cordless phones, wideband systems). The Eureka IHS participants involve major European consumer electronics firms (Electrolux, GEC, Mullard, Philips, Siemens, Thomson, Thorn-EMI), most of whom are involved in producing demonstration projects around a number of *trigger applications*.

The triggers currently prioritised by the IHS programme include: video and audio distribution, telecontrol and monitoring, security, and shared resources for home computers.[21] The programme aims to demonstrate these trigger applications by 1989, and to subsequently coordinate marketing—by means such as a common logo for products, making it clear to consumers that the devices will interwork.

It remains to be seen how divergent in practice the North American and European (and Japanese) home automation programmes will be, and how far the different regional strategies will lead to universally applicable systems—or indeed, systems particularly suitable for their own markets. What is apparent, however, is that the issue of technical standards is again a central one. In this instance, it is quite possible that the interconnect standards for home devices will have to be related to the standards being negotiated for computer communications in general—Open Systems Interconnection.

Many applications will clearly require linking home systems to the PSTN—for example emergency alarms and other data communications. Thus, some minimal conformity to these standards will probably be required.

Let us then consider possible application areas in more detail, and see what these may imply for the future development of HI. Three types of application seem to be of most significance for the development of 'smart houses', whether of the North American, Japanese or European varieties: security systems, energy management (and other domestic work), and entertainment. While these application areas are in many respects convergent, as we shall see, they differ in terms of their requirements for domestic data networks.

We have already devoted some attention in this chapter to home entertainment and home security systems. These have very different requirements for media, since large volumes of data transmission are required to relay high-quality audio and video material around the home, while the signals involved in security applications are much less complex and need not be continuous.

The decreasing costs of stand-alone audio and video devices may mitigate against installation of the cable systems that seem best suited to disseminate entertainment around the home. Why not simply install radios, hi-fis, TVs in different rooms (or carry them around)? Three main incentives for inter-communication in the entertainment sphere can be specified:

— the ability to follow the same broadcast or recorded material as one moves around the house, or as household members are dispersed in different areas—without loss of quality or continuity, and without needing to carry the data storage medium around;
— the ability to follow both recorded and broadcast material, without needing to devote time to manually operating equipment (since devices can simply be turned on and off without tuning, etc., or can even be operated on default by proximity);
— and the ability to use the media to communicate with household members, to take external messages, or to display other household information.

Some consumer electronics companies have already begun to offer programmable networked home entertainment systems that fulfil some of these functions and thus move away from traditional 'stand-alone' or 'rack' systems. For example, Bang and Olufsen's Link System offers TV monitors and loudspeakers dispersed around the home, with wall-mounted control panels in each room that can be operated via a handset (described in recent advertising copy as a 'conductor's baton with which to orchestrate a symphony around your home').[22] Among the features promoted for this set of products are the ability to upgrade basic units into a full-fledged system, and the ability to programme the system in order to automatically turn on or off in particular rooms (so as to function, for example, as an early-morning alarm).

Alarm and security applications, which feature frequently in 'smart house' proposals, typically do not require such high speeds and volumes of data transmission; the information produced by such equipment is much more limited and standardised. The exceptions here are video cameras installed for security purposes—these may seem rather extravagant for domestic applications, but are already in use in some apartment blocks.

Even more so than in the case of entertainment, there is a strong practical incentive to move away from stand-alone to integrated systems (as long as these are secure) here; why duplicate alarms, and why not make sure that alarms can be seen or heard wherever one is? It also makes sense to provide alarms with more distant communications facilities. Some devices can issue alarms by telephoning specified authorities or the owner; others can be interrogated from a distance, for example, to check if windows have been unlocked or devices turned off. Most of the data requirements here could be handled by a combination of mains signalling, radio and telephony, if new household networks were not installed for other purposes.

Security concerns are particularly apparent in the development of 'smart buildings' for industrial or office use. Fire and smoke detectors and access-control systems are featured, along with communications and energy management facilities, in the Honeywell integrated buildings (such as the Seattle First National Bank); Honeywell forecasts that a third of new office-type buildings will follow such a model by the mid-1990s.[23]

Of course, HI based on costly minicomputers such as these buildings employ is not feasible; but homes are smaller and require less elaborate facilities than office buildings, and microcomputer power is rapidly attaining levels restricted to minicomputers in the past. Indeed, some advanced security HI devices like those discussed above are already available as prototypes or hi-tech luxuries.[24] As technology transfer from industry becomes more feasible, as IHS standards diffuse and as 'smart house' systems move into mass production, it will be increasingly simple to build in facilities that allow sensing equipment (detectors) to intercommunicate with communication devices (emergency alarm buttons and other household appliances), and other types of medical alarm system.

The last of the three main areas of application noted above is also the site of considerable development effort—*energy management system*. Mains signalling research has been pioneered by electricity companies, whose interests have been twofold: first, remote metering would speed up charging for power consumption and cut labour requirements; and second, it would allow for efforts to regulate demand (and thus smooth out the peaks in power use that require large amounts of extra generating capacity) by means of a more flexible tariff structure.

'Smart' meters would contribute to these goals in several ways. They would allow meters to be read without the need for meter readers to physically visit homes (or to ask users to cooperate in assessing their consumption). If suitably equipped with displays (and even more advanced facilities), they would allow users to estimate far more effectively the costs of particular decisions concerning when and how to use appliances. And they would be able to respond to tariff changes, issuing mains signals to instruct domestic appliances to operate or not, according to current power costs. This would permit energy companies to introduce more complicated tariff structures to manage loads more effectively. Existing timers, as featured on central heating systems and some stoves, for example, already permit a measure of programming to operate at off-peak electricity tariffs; but these are far less flexible than 'informed' systems would be.

The monitoring and control of equipment for energy management purposes can be a trigger for other types of remote monitoring and control, pursued for purposes of convenience, security and comfort. In particular, it is likely that there will be an integration of heat control/air conditioning systems with devices for ventilation and maintaining air quality (note the emerging health concerns around domestic pollution from radon and the vapour discharges of chipboard and other furniture). More generally, the development of distant control facilities for white goods may be an important step towards the application of IHS to housework: for example, users being able to instruct cookers to begin to prepare meals while they are still on their way home.

Although not all of the features of 'smart house' programmes have such obvious utility as energy management, and although the developments at present seem to be supply-driven rather than market-based, the 'trigger services' that are being actively developed by potential suppliers should be taken seriously. It is likely that many of the facilities offered by these systems will prove attractive to groups of consumers. And some of these functions will also attract some service and utility authorities, such as welfare services for the elderly (emergency alarms) and electricity companies (energy management). Thus the diffusion and continued development of components of home automation is extremely likely over the next years and decades. This is liable to lead to innovations in a range of new and complementary household goods and services to consumers. (For example, the possibility arises of malfunctioning devices communicating directly with manufacturers or retailers for diagnostic and maintenance instructions.)

We have noted three main areas where in-home communication systems are being developed. How might these relate together, given their different characteristics? Figure 6.1 presents a schema for the possible evolution of such systems towards integrated IHS, taking into account the technical and demand factors noted above, especially the different requirements of various applications for communications capacity. The 'smart house' programmes may speed up the move towards total integration of networked home devices; otherwise, we are likely to witness slow and uneven integration of specific types of equipment, in particular entertainment and housework systems.

The speed and form of innovation and diffusion of such HI will be affected by numerous factors. These include extremely broad aspects of social change.

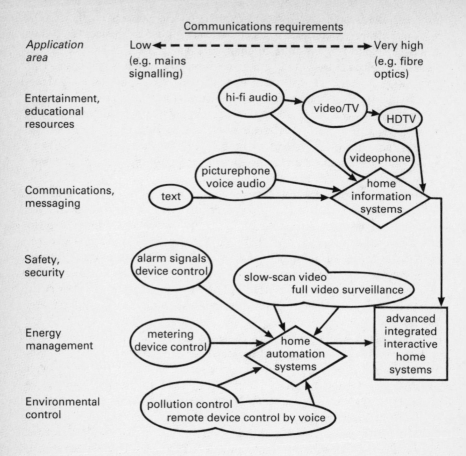

Figure 6.1 Requirements and prospects for interactive home systems

For example, high levels of dualism and inequality in society, with a very uneven distribution of income and of new equipment, are liable to lead to more emphasis, perhaps, on security systems for the elite, mass entertainment for the relatively deprived. Likewise, high levels of social and geographical mobility may lead to more turnover in housing stock and equipment, and thus facilitate more rapid innovation. Other factors are more to do with 'narrow' policy decisions on 'technical' issues—for example, agreements on standards for home communications devices. And some are to do with relatively limited social policies—for example, the choice of various methods that might be used for monitoring the well-being of the elderly (which is a choice that will probably be highly conditioned by policies on residential provisions for such social groups).

While the widespread diffusion of home networks is liable to be a long-term prospect, several types of technological development (some of them no doubt accelerated by 'smart house' initiatives) are likely to diffuse widely more immediately. Among these are:

— improvements in the safety and security of electrical and other equipment;
— devices (lights, heating, etc.) that are operated on the basis of responses to room occupancy or to the action of other devices (e.g. video graphics to accompany music);
— improved energy conservation systems, probably coupled with ventilation and anti-pollution equipment;
— further developments in remote control and monitoring of equipment;
— more elaborate forms of electronic interpersonal communication;
— the linkage of all sorts of domestic equipment to remote individuals and information services though the ISDN.

We can also anticipate the emergence of a variety of new social concerns surrounding these developments, for example conflicts over technical standards, and worries about privacy and civil liberties as more features of private life can (in principle) be monitored remotely by authorities, neighbours, etc. We shall consider some of the issues that are raised by the widespread adoption of HI in the following chapter.

Notes

1. It should be stressed that it is only the interactivity with the technology that is being discussed here. In using 'passive entertainment' devices, people are not really passive: even the lone viewer is engaged in an act of construction in appreciating the programmes, and where a group is involved there may well be intense interaction concerning the content of the medium.
2. There is little analysis of these developments, but see Buckles (1987) for a first stab.
3. See Defanti (1984).
4. *CD-I News*, October 1987. The system is expected to be launched in autumn 1988; the CD system conforms to yet another set of standards than CD-I and DVI, ICVD (Interactive Compact Video Disc).
5. *CD-I News*, October 1987.
6. See articles in the May 1985 issue of *IEEE Spectrum*.
7. Reported in 'Exercise Freaks can count on Curly', *The Guardian* (London), 7 February 1986.
8. Quoted from an advertisement in *Innovation—The Catalogue*, Christmas 1987. (This is a document well worth following for intelligence on what mail order shopping groups consider to be marketable consumer technology.)
9. The most serious application of simple robotics to the home is in utilities for disabled people—devices that can remotely open doors or windows, for example. These devices are rarely real robotics, more often simple servomotors that can be remotely activated or triggered by environmental changes. They may be important in bringing IT control of motor equipment into the home. For a contrary view—from an entrepreneur actively engaged in this area—that 'personal

robotics' will be a major area of HI, see Pawson's interview with Schofield (1987b).

10. Schofield (1984).

11. Some psycheware described by Schofield (1984) is rather sinister: for example, one system adds subliminal messages to TV or video material; as well as self-control messages aimed at increasing self-confidence, etc., there are offerings intended to produce sexual arousal (presumably in someone other than the owner of the programme . . . and quite possibly someone who is unaware of its being used).

12. For example, Feigenbaum and McCorduck (1983), promoters of the 'fifth generation', seem to think that this is one of its main selling points.

13. Such as those novels of John Brunner, Philip K. Dick, William Gibson and Stanislaw Lem which deal with the long-term implications of IT, moving well beyond earlier (but often still worthy) fictional studies of the problems associated with 'electronic brains' and intelligent robots.

14. Watts (1986). One recent journalist's account of 'self-monitoring equipment' included biofeedback devices and audio tapes for relaxation, heartbeat monitors, wristwatches and hand-held pulse-rate monitors, and blood pressure monitors. Additionally, among health systems for home computers, 'Your Health' for Sinclair Spectrum and Amstrad machines sets out to diagnose dietary imbalance on the basis of users' input of information on their meals and their personal characteristics.

15. Bates (1986).

16. For an interesting discussion of developments here, see Blackburn *et al.* (1986).

17. Schofield (1984).

18. Reported by Whymant (1987).

19. This section draws on Tom Bowling's (1986) presentation to the Home Informatics Workshop in London, November 1986. The National Association of Homebuilders involves over 130,000 companies, responsible for over 90 per cent of domestic, light commercial and industrial construction in the United States. Following the London Workshop, a 'Home of the Future' project, along similar (but less ambitious) lines to the US smart house programme, was launched by a group of British companies—including construction firms and utilities.

20. This discussion draws upon verbal presentations made by Erik Bates and Clive Weston to the Home Informatics Workshop. A useful source of news on home automation is *Home Bus Info*; a newsletter produced by Sala Communications of Amsterdam. A recent collection of essays on technical and strategic issues in IHS is NEDO (1987).

21. It will be interesting to observe Philips' strategies here: as well as its Eureka involvement, it is involved with Sony on CD systems, and is also a member of the US smart house project!

22. Bang and Olufsen promotional leaflet, distributed in 1986 by Bang and Olufsen UK.

23. Watts (1986).

24. Again, see articles in the May 1985 issue of *IEEE Spectrum*.

7 Home Informatics and information society

7.1 Some key themes

Let us summarise some of the key issues about the development of HI raised by the preceding chapters. First, while HI is regarded sceptically by many commentators, and remains a peripheral consideration in most government IT policies, we have seen that it is the focus of considerable effort on the part of a range of industries. They recognise HI as a potential source of new markets, one that is likely to be increasingly important in international competition. There is good reason to believe that some of these industrial hopes are justified, even though it is difficult to forecast demand for new HI products, and the future evolution of markets is a matter of great uncertainty.

Second, there are lessons that can be drawn from experiences with IT goods and services over the last decade, and there is evidence that some of these lessons are being drawn—though perhaps not widely enough. The role of technical standards in facilitating diffusion—and cutting out some competitors—is one issue that is being recognised. Another is the relation between HI, on the one hand, and the telecommunications and broadcasting systems that can deliver information and services useful to consumers to the home. Policies for the development of telecommunications infrastructure are liable to be key determinants in influencing the rate and shape of HI development. The provision of network infrastructure may be difficult to evaluate in conventional economic terms, given the uncertain size of new markets and the many externalities that may be involved, but HI means that telecommunications and industrial policy will be increasingly intertwined. And given that an important area for HI development is providing entertainment and other information services, we may also expect to see mass media and broadcasting policies entangled with telecommunications and industrial policy. Established media policies, already under challenge from developments in satellite broadcasting and cable, are liable to face radical new challenges.

Third, IT is making possible new commercial interventions, and even trade, in services that have previously been 'protected'—or better, 'insulated'—from foreign or private competition. This insulation has been provided by the traditional, local-level production of many services, by national borders, and by government regulations, rather than primarily economic considerations of a classical protectionist kind. HI may thus raise new trade issues in services as well as in the field of consumer goods, if the market for services to HI equipment (whether delivered by telecommunications or data storage techniques) grows. The issues raised may be particularly difficult to resolve, since they raise problems of cultural and welfare policy. In turn, the future path of development of HI itself is liable to be shaped in substantial ways by IT strategies pursued by Welfare State organisations—and the role of the Welfare State may well be challenged by private innovations in HI.

These points indicate that considerably more, and more systematic, attention should be paid to HI, and by a much wider body of informed opinion. In many instances, there is a basic lack of information (or a lack of awareness of what information there is) concerning key topics. These topics include, for example, product development, the setting of standards, the shape of existing markets, the stance of different sectors of industry and branches of government, and the relevance of trade and related international negotiations. This severely curtails the possibilities for informed policy debate about the narrow concerns that emerge around HI, let alone the wider concerns about its broad social and economic implications.

This study has set out to provide relevant information and to raise pertinent questions, rather than to provide solutions to the challenges posed by HI. However, we can conclude with an appraisal of outstanding challenges, which can be grouped according to three types of concern. First, there are concerns about economic implications of HI: are there substantial markets here? what is required for national or regional producers to capitalise on them? If these are concerns about missing out on the potential economic benefits of HI developments, the second set of concerns focuses on the possibilities of sections of society missing out on the potential social benefits of using HI. Are we moving towards a world in which we see new divisions between the information-rich and the information-poor? Will the traditional goals of universality and equity supposedly embodied in welfare states (and public telecommunications utilities) be undermined by new private enterprises? Third, there are concerns that focus less on capturing and spreading benefits of HI than on avoiding social and psychological costs held to be associated with the new technologies. Will the interactivity of HI lead to an impoverishment of human interaction? Is the attractiveness of HI to individual consumers outweighed by more general social problems that may be associated with its diffusion?

7.2 HI, growth and competitiveness

Several commentators have argued that IT makes possible a recovery from the world economic problems of the 1970s and 1980s, or, more locally, that appropriate IT strategies would make possible a new European renaissance. Mackintosh (1986), for example, argues that the establishment of a broadband European telecommunications grid is an essential element in regaining European industrial strength (he uses the term 'renaissance'), and that consumer goods and services are areas whose growth could be triggered in this way. Freeman and Perez (1986) talk about new 'technological para-digms', patterns of economic organisation based on clusters of interconnected technologies which constitute the common sense about what best-practice production is. Revolutionary technological change, such as is associated with IT, allows for new paradigms to be constructed, in which not only are industrial processes redesigned, but markets are also restructured with new methods of social organisation that make use of new products. Gershuny (1986) extends these arguments about infrastructure and technological paradigms with rather more attention to the potential for final demand growth.[1]

Pessimistic views of the long-term impact of IT on employment, suggest-ing that there will be major displacement of labour as new technologies diffuse through the formal economy, often imply that human needs have basically been satisfied by existing goods and services. In this case, new production processes can be seen as liable to displace labour by increasing the efficiency of existing operations. This view is accurate in so far as it depicts the exhaustion of (or saturation of demand within) a technological paradigm. But if revolutionary new technologies make new technological paradigms possible, then new ways of satisfying final consumption requirements may be created—and new consumption requirements along with them. Gershuny argues that technological innovation in industry may indeed increase efficien-cy and reduce hours of work (note that this may take the form of unemployment, or of reductions in the working lifetime); that the new time freed from formal work is liable to be translated into consumption demands for more or new goods and services; and that consumers may also seek goods and services to free the time spent in informal work (he notes in this context the upward trend in time devoted to shopping and shopping-related travel, and suggests opportunities for teleshopping). Investment in infrastructure (and, we might add, efforts to reconcile technical standards) would provide opportunities for new demand to manifest through a shift in technological paradigm.

If even only a small sample of the range of innovations discussed in previous chapters actually finds application in the home, this would be a substantial transformation of household equipment. And it seems likely that rather a large proportion of these innovations are likely to find mass markets—let alone the many others which no doubt we lack the imagination to pinpoint! Thus, changes in the household economy in the next decades are liable to be as significant as those occurring in the post-war decades—which were associated with great changes in our ways of life.

Whether these changes will lead to the same sort of economic virtuous circle as was apparent in the post-war boom—where, for example, new living patterns associated with automobiles and white goods underpinned demand for construction and related industries—is less certain. The new consumer goods and services associated with IT are liable to open up large new areas of demand, but it is by no means clear that these will feed back into employment in the way described for previous technological paradigms. The new products rarely require labour-intensive manufacture, and it is not immediately apparent that new ways of life around HI would call for supporting expansion of formal employment.[2]

A new technological paradigm does not automatically mean full employment—although we should remember that the concept of full employment is not really static, and that lifetime hours of work determine the relationship between the level of employment and the demand for labour. But whether there are resources available to provide adequate living standards depends upon three factors: (1) are there markets that can be exploited? (2) are local producers in a position to exploit—and to want to exploit these markets? And (3) are state agencies (or other institutions we could imagine) in a position to redistribute—or to want to redistribute—the proceeds of this production?

If we accept that there are liable to be large markets for HI products, then it is the two subsequent questions that must concern us. While they are often regarded as contradictory—taxing successful industries is like killing the goose that laid the golden egg—this is far too simplistic. Government expenditure on infrastructure, training and direct redistribution does help structure markets and often reduces costs of production. The more pertinent question is probably how far these effects benefit national producers rather than those of competing countries: does increased consumer expenditure go on imports? Will the new telecommunications infrastructure be used predominantly to convey services produced elsewhere? Tax burdens are only one of a large number of determinants of the competitiveness of national manufacturing and service industries. And one of the main messages of this study is that a failure to be competitive in HI may put a country—or region—at a severe disadvantage in the emerging global economy.

Among the determinants of competitiveness that are liable to prove crucial in the HI sphere are:

— *Marketing.* Innovations that fail to meet changing market requirements are doomed to failure. Marketing of HI products requires a lot more than jumping on the bandwagon of IT hyperbole (repackaging existing products as hi-tech). It requires research into market trends and the social processes that underlie these, analysis of successful and unsuccessful innovations, attention to social experiments that can reveal ripe sites for IT applications, and the development of strategies that take into account the issues of consumer confidence raised in Chapter 3 (e.g. the role of future proofing, the role of common standards).

— *Awareness.* There have been a remarkable number of occasions where suppliers have been wrongfooted by competitors unveiling new and advanced solutions to familiar problems. In many of the sectors that HI impinges upon there seems to be remarkable complacency concerning the pace of technological change, and efforts to spread awareness of potential applications to their activities need to be fostered.

— *Training*. In some countries at least—Britain is an oft-cited example—the problems of awareness are compounded by relatively low levels of management technical expertise, and training for the workforce in general, that would enable more flexible response and more innovatory solutions to changing market conditions and production processes.
Cooperation. This is a theme that arises in several guises, as we have seen: competitors and groups from different industrial sectors may need to cooperate in order to establish common technical standards; governments and national industries may need to cooperate in order to mount costly R&D programmes or social experiments, or to establish markets of sufficient scale to compete in global terms. The 'convergence' associated with IT is liable to increase the need for both forms of cooperation.

We have argued that HI is an area—or, rather, a complex of areas—of industrial activity in which national competitiveness will be critical to national economic prospects. In other words, performance in this sphere will be a key to the level of participation that can be attained in the global information society. In this case the problems associated with HI are a matter of how to play an important role in its creation. Let us now turn our attention to a related question that poses itself *within* national societies, for problems of unequal participation in 'information society' are also posed by the trajectories of HI.

7.3 HI and dualism

We have avoided the use of phrases such as 'the impact of technology' or 'technological determinants of social change'. Technological change is a significant feature of broader social evolution, and is not one that can be wished away or one that is totally pliable to social interests. Rather, technological developments—especially those such as are involved in a technological revolution like that associated with IT—provide social interests with new opportunities to affect the social and physical worlds. (And this includes opportunities to shape further technological developments.)

New 'technological paradigms', from this viewpoint, are the product of social agents choosing to develop some of the potentials offered by technological revolutions. Previous paradigms have been developed in line with what are sometimes termed particular regimes of social regulation;[3] thus the mass production and new leading products of the post-war boom period depended for their success on the creation of mass markets. In turn, this involved the establishment of specific wage systems, of credit in new forms, of Welfare State policies (with income support, new service employment, etc.). It likewise seems probable that the development of new mass markets—for HI products in particular— will be strongly affected by policies for full employment and/or the redistribution of work and income. The size and shape of consumer markets will depend upon disposable income and leisure time. Furthermore, without redistributive policies, a more dualistic society may well emerge from changes in the formal economy.[4] If greater dualism is a feature of emerging technological paradigms, two consequences are likely: first, segmentation of consumption patterns (accompanying segmentation in labour markets), perhaps between 'high culture' for the elite, 'bread and circuses' for the masses; second, greater insecurity and social conflict, with more emphasis on means of social control and private security, including those based on IT (hi-tech policing and private anti-crime and personal protection systems).

In the event of greater dualism emerging in the formal economy, and not being counteracted by social and other policies, then the development pattern of HI would be moulded by the structure of markets thus established. Additionally, HI—in particular, access to useful sources of data, access to resources for planning one's life circumstances—would probably be used in order to reinforce these inequalities, thus justifying fears of divisions between the 'information-rich' and '-poor'. As well as the more privileged social groups being able to exercise more control over their own circumstances by such means, they would also be in a position to do what elites always do: to reproduce themselves by passing on advantages to their children. Apart from purely financial advantages, there would be advantages based on information-richness. Improved educational opportunities from the use of HI for educational purposes—video game-like learning packages on home computers, instructive and engrossing interactive encyclopedias on CD-I, tutorials delivered over telecommunications systems. Improved health and fitness from the application of HI in the form of medical monitoring equipment, exercise and biofeedback systems, expert systems for diagnosis and advice on lifestyles, remote medical counselling and tele-diagnosis, and so on.

Whether or not HI is applied in order to reinforce an emerging class structure, it is very likely that major areas of HI activity will concern services that have heretofore, in large part because of their requirements for interactivity, been provided in labour-intensive ways as collective, public services—large components of health, education and even welfare activities. We have already sketched in many of the technological developments relevant to this prospect (for instance, in Chapter 6). Table 7.1 sets out a number of social trends that make it likely that the technological opportunities present here will be seized upon. The upshot may well be that public services in the coming decades will find themselves under the same sort of challenge from new, private modes of provision, based on new consumer goods and services, as did such traditional services as laundry, domestic service, cinema and theatre, and bus and train transport in the post-war period.

Now, competition is not in itself a bad thing: and it may well stimulate innovation in services that are in some ways hidebound, bureaucratic, and

Table 7.1   IT innovations as challenging public services

New modes of provision (often IT-using and private) may be *facilitated* by:

— public concerns for self-help and preventative medicine, 'whole foods', sport and physical fitness, 'alternative' education and health;
— an associated blurring of boundaries between medical and lifestyle, sport and dietary, care and leisure concerns, with a more 'holistic' approach to health that takes into account psychological (and even spiritual) wellbeing alongside physical fitness, and to education that includes emotional as well as intellectual development;
— critiques of collective provision of welfare services, arguing that they are (inevitably?) bureaucratic and sometimes inhumanely managed, foster dependency, encourage wasteful attitudes and even frauds, run up high costs through poor (and oversized) management;
— entrepreneurial moves from a wide spectrum of commercial interests, ranging from privatisation of conventional services (schools, hospitals) to new 'alternative' and 'complementary' approaches to health care and schooling, and from sports centres to wholefood shops;
— increased willingness to pay for security measures, especially in a more dualistic and crime-ridden scenario;
— and political ferment, with central government seeking greater control over many activities (local government, educational curricula, etc.) and to promote market solutions to welfare issues.

New modes of provision may *undermine* public services by:

— a draining-off of many of the more articulate and innovation-promoting clients (to make use of) and staff (to work for) the new services;
— increasing real and perceived inequities in public service resourcing, delivery, and outcomes, resulting from improved use of the traditional services by those who are also using the new services (children of 'informatised' parents, patients with print-outs of health trends);
— a perception of the traditional services as tatty and second-rate, and as not displaying quality improvements visible in other sectors of the economy (although continuing to demand high levels of expenditure), which is liable to undermine willingness to invest in them;
— a growing market for private services offering complete packages combining traditional and IT-based elements of provision;
— and shifts in public conceptions of the nature of, and of rights in, welfare, quality of life, education and health, which may intensify criticism of public provisions and intensify support for alternatives.

Table 7.2   Constraints to IT innovation in public services

- stringent *financial limits* in the existing economic climate in many countries;
- difficulties in assessing, in many social services, the 'impact' of interventions or the 'productivity' of workers, which make it hard to *cost-justify* some categories of expenditure;
- the problems of *recruiting* or retaining technically skilled personnel in public services at civil service wages, (these have dogged and delayed a number of ambitious computerisation programmes in the United Kingdom);
- the *divisions of responsibility* and effective authority between local government and different branches of the Welfare State, which may obstruct the interchange of data, and economies of scale such as the coordinated acquisition of IT, agreement on general standards and strategies, and the sharing of training provisions and advice facilities;
- the structural tendencies of *bureaucracies*, who are liable to develop their own self-interested 'corporate' goals and mission definitions, reducing democratic accountability and stifling 'grass-root' initiatives (including those that might facilitate wider dissemination of information, interactive services, or IT innovations appropriate to particular client groups);
- the high 'personal service' components of many education and health services— which mitigate against standardised systems although they are often amenable to more flexible microelectronics-based innovations—but which also make *client acceptance* of and adaptation to technological change important in facilitating or inhibiting innovation;
- public and professional concerns, about protection of the *privacy* of individual data and against increased surveillance of the citizen;
- more recent concerns about *data and system security*, the damage that might be inflicted by hackers and computer saboteurs to official databases;
- the convergence of technologies and potential interdependence of systems that this enables, raising issues of *standards* and *networking procedures* between different devices and software systems (as well as intensifying concerns about privacy and security);
- and, in common with many other organisations, difficulties posed by the *pace of IT innovation*, such as: the pressure of many competing demands for expenditure; uncertainty about the obsolescence of systems; a tendency to defer decisions until the next generation comes along; and difficulty in keeping up to date and well informed.

deserving of other widespread criticisms. But, as Table 7.1 also goes on to outline, the sorts of innovation that we have been discussing provide a severe challenge to public services. They may well intensify inequalities in welfare provisions and outcomes (another reinforcement of social dualism) and lead to public provision of welfare services coming to be seen as an inferior service, unattractive both to taxpayers and potential employees.

Although providers of many of these services often feel beleaguered already, by restrictions on their budgets and criticism from their political masters and mistresses, there will be no escaping these challenges. They will require proactive innovation policies by welfare and educational authorities, making their own use of IT to improve the effectiveness and quality of their services, and taking account of the trends that emerge in HI. There are severe constraints faced by would-be innovators in public services (Table 7.2), who will rarely be able to play a dominant role in establishing technological trajectories (unless profound political changes take place), so that it is quite likely that we shall see a new coevolution (symbiosis or competition?) of public and private services. Ensuring that this does not reinforce dualism within 'information societies' will be a major task of the coming decades.

In large part, the steps necessary for public service providers and clients to be able to seize the opportunities of IT in a proactive way—rather than as a reactive response to competition from private market developments—are similar to those outlined at the end of Section 7.3. In other words, better training in and awareness of technological facilities, more cooperation between agencies whose traditional separation is undermined by 'convergence', and better 'marketing' of their services are important. On this last point, there would seem to be two possible paths: one route is to treat the users of public services as clients to whom the services are being marketed, and to engage in better market research to establish their changing needs and preferences; the other route is to involve the users as active participants in the shaping of services, involving them in major choices by such means as community health councils and popular planning fora. One route is more technocratic, one more democratic: either (or perhaps best, a combination of both) is liable to give rise to a wider range of innovative inputs to public services than relying on service professionals alone for this.[5]

7.4 HI and ways of life

What, then, of ways of life more generally? To start with the issue that is closest to home, as it were—what of the implications of HI for housework? Most of the innovations we have discussed can improve the quality of domestic work, both in terms of the convenience and effort required, and in terms of the quality of the product of the work. Skilled household tasks—cooking, some types of repair and cleaning, dressmaking, etc.—may be 'deskilled' by 'smart' apparatus and access to training, advice and instruction made available in the form of new information services supplied via online or data storage systems. This would enable more people to use the equipment effectively, and perhaps reinforce the gradual tendency for men to engage in routine domestic work and for women to engage in non-routine DIY-type activities. Furthermore, it would be likely to increase the tendency of some types of activity to become more specialist or hobby-like (e.g. gourmet versus routine meals), and for some types of informal work to become more leisure-like (e.g. childcare, travel, shopping).

Some savings in domestic work time may also be apparent, however. Many of these would be in 'domestic travel': not only shopping (especially if teleshopping develops successfully), but also within-home travel as devices can be operated remotely or carried around. Other savings would be associated with greater convenience of equipment and related products (such as microwaves and convenience foods). But the most significant developments will be not the purely quantitative ones in the volume of domestic work, but the qualitative ones.

Particularly important here are liable to be:

— the sexual redivision of labour between men and women in families (e.g. men being more prepared to use hi-tech and low-skill white goods, women to use informatised power tools);
— the relaxation of the necessity for people to be physically proximate to make use of common goods and services (e.g. the reputed shift away from family meals as a consequence of the use of microwave cookers which allow any family member to reheat food at any time);
— the use of HI to reduce the need for investment of human time in some personal care and interpersonal communications activities (with the possible loss of important categories of contact and stimulation for some social groups, e.g. small children, elderly relatives, the isolated and marginal);
— and the 'blurring' of distinctions between traditionally separate categories of household activity (e.g. housework and leisure, personal care and sport, entertainment and education).

Beyond the housework issue, we have noted two types of problem that are frequently raised when the broader implications of IT in general and HI in particular for our ways of life are considered. One problem concerns security, privacy and civil liberties. If more households are linked into communications networks, then it is conceivable that 'hackers' will make their way into domestic systems—perhaps disrupting them, perhaps spying on them. (And the hackers might be joined in the latter activity by tax and police agencies, in the same way that telephones may now be tapped.) It is possible to determine the outputs of conventional VDUs from outside the buildings housing them; there has been concern about the insecurity of business information handled in this way, and it is easy to imagine such concern extending to consumer applications.

A second set of concerns relates to the potential for a retrogressive substitution of interactivity with IT for human interaction. Chapter 6 speculated about the prospects for IT-based displacement of some forms of social intercourse: the problems that this might raise include:

— an impairment of capacities to relate to real people whose 'messy' habits and problems may require more effort—if posing more challenges that can provoke self-development—than would interacting with ever-interested, ever-supportive, ever-interesting IT substitutes;

— growing implicit assumptions that there is no real need on the part of other people for inputs from and the physical (as contrasted, say, with the telecommunicated) presence of oneself, and an associated tendency to reduce one's availability for, say, elderly relatives and neighbours;

— dependence upon the fantasy world of, say, video games for one's adventure and sense of achievement, upon feedback from, say, IT 'comforters' and pets, for one's self-esteem and sense of being positively regarded by others:

— associated with the above, a growing mismatch between individual mental models of the social world and the nature and meaning of one's actions within it;

— and, at a more collective level, the formation of subcultures sharing mutual interests but progressively withdrawing from more than superficial contact with other social groups, leading to a lack of mutual understanding, greater potential for conflict, etc.

Each of these dangers seems to be a possible tendency associated with IT and especially HI development, although some of them are probably much further away than others. They are certainly important problems to guard against, and tend to give the lie to those optimistic commentators who expect information society to be all sweetness and light, for IT to solve social problems.[6] (Often the introduction of more new technology is heralded as the means of resolving problems associated with the introduction of earlier technology.) It is not good enough to simply point to possible IT applications that can alleviate social problems, e.g. consumer and social service versions of the interactive videodiscs now being used by firms, for example, to train workers in developing attitudes supportive of health and safety, which could be used to teach people how to detect and intervene in, say, the social isolation of elderly or infirm people. (Indeed, an interactive videodisc has been designed in an effort to help young people in Northern Ireland overcome prejudices deriving from the longstanding communal conflict into which they have been born.) IT can be used as part of strategies to alleviate social problems, but it is far from being a panacea: and it is just as likely to be used in innovative ways that will give rise to new problems or intensify existing ones (as in the intensification of exploitative sexual practices that appears to be associated with video media and now viewdata—e.g. Minitel Rose sections of Teletel: see Chapter 4).

At the present stage of development, for every real or hypothetical danger associated with the new technology a real or hypothetical benefit can be cited. There is no way of knowing how these costs and benefits will combine in the future—especially since people are liable to pursue individual benefits at the risk of generating externalities in the form of collective costs, and to find innovative ways of compensating for if not overcoming those costs that are imposed on them in turn. The task of forecasting, as we have often had cause to note, is as foredoomed as it is necessary in such circumstances. It is necessary in part because our response to the emergence of costs and benefits cannot be to lapse into futurological optimism or intellectual pessimism. It is necessary to struggle to find ways of minimising costs and maximising benefits, of course, and to argue for and bring to bear principles of justice and equity which give content to otherwise empty concepts of optimisation.

Who can be the key actors here? While some of the best-informed people concerning matters of technological development are entrepreneurs and private sector managers, the interests of these groups—however well-meaning they may be as individuals—are rarely sufficiently representative of the range of social groups in emerging information societies for the rest of us to feel completely confident in entrusting them with envisioning and shaping the future. The same is true of the (generally less well-informed, it must be admitted) academic and intellectual elites, valuable though their debates may be. Wider debate is required: this means that the arguments in earlier sections about the need for training, awareness, cooperation, etc. have to be extended very broadly, to encompass local authorities, social movements, consumer groups, trade unions, school and college students, self-help organisations of marginalised communities, and the like.

What sorts of strategies may be employed by these 'everyday' actors; they are not policymakers, in the position of being able to draw up national or corporate strategies? Four quite distinctive—though not necessarily exclusive —types of strategies may be identified.[7]

A first approach is *reformism*: to seek through organised activity to influence policymakers, or to arouse public opinion or affected elites so as to influence policymakers. Here the goals may be to effect specific policies—e.g. regulation of media content, ensuring public access to services—or to change policy styles—e.g. to obtain consultation of community groups in the case of the development of telecommunications infrastructure. Reformism requires the presence of large-scale social movements or committed pressure groups with a strong interest in IT-related issues in order to be effective. In information society reformism may flourish as access to data and communications resources allows communities of interest to form rapidly; but the pace of change may be such that, without foresight capabilities, reformism will be always finding itself trailing behind hydra-headed problems.

A contrasting approach is *contestation*: to attempt to overturn existing power structures and thus to restructure the nature of policies and policy-making. This approach usually involves militant mobilisation of groups on the 'receiving end': something that is easier to do when the problems are concentrated and easily related to a particular programme, such as the construction of a nuclear power station or the close-down of a factory. It may be an approach that can capitalise on the divisions of a dualistic information society, although it is probable that in this scenario marginalised groups would be fragmented and often pitted against each other, and the dangers of sectarianism and self-righteous authoritarianism that have dogged radical groups would remain present.

Two other modes of action are less a matter of collective action. *Social responsibility* simply involves the exercise of individual choice: boycotting classes of goods and services on principled grounds (and encouraging others to do so), 'whistle-blowing' about abuses of power (such as unauthorised telephone tapping). This sort of action can alert public opinion and have a demonstration effect: however, it typically requires individual resources (financial, psychological, and even technical), and is most effective if related to a reformist or contestatory social movement. It is less likely to be effective in a dualistic society where identification with the actions of people on the other side of social divides may be more difficult.

Finally, *counter cultural activity* involves groups of people following alternative lifestyles, often detaching themselves from many of the economic and political institutions of the wider society. Such actions may again have demonstration effects (although, as has so often happened with youth cultures, superficial aspects of the lifestyles may be commercialised and drained of substance). It is certainly conceivable that innovations in, for example, the use of IT for work organisation (e.g. 'computer-mediated cooperative work'), for community communications (perhaps like Geonet's 'Green' electronic network), and in leisure activities (new uses of new media) might be promoted via what begins as counter cultural action. But counter cultures often run the risk of being vanguards: they may be singled out for repression without evoking much public support, and if information society involves a proliferation of more self-contained groups, this may be a serious risk.

The point of this discussion has not been to recommend one strategy: all four can draw upon good supporting arguments, and in practice we are bound to see elements of each. The purpose has been to demonstrate that there are numerous ways by which relatively powerless social actors can try to change the course of social and technological development. It cannot be guaranteed that these efforts will head off the worst fears raised by the development of HI: but the only reason to think that they will only have limited effect on what new technological paradigms emerge is that debate and discussion of the new technologies remains so limited. It would be ironic indeed if a lack of information prevented wider social participation in shaping information society.

7.5 Concluding notes

This chapter has been dwelling on problems that may be associated with HI, not in order to argue against the development of these applications of IT, but in order to raise awareness of issues that need to be confronted in shaping this development. Table 7.3 recapitulates these problems and others raised in this study.

Table 7.3   Critical issues facing 'information society'

— How far will inequalities in access to domestic equipment and private services be replicated around the new technologies, and, if they are to a considerable extent, what will be the consequences in terms of service content and quality?

— How far will the developments be driven by the growth of private markets, and how far by the activities of public service agencies with some redistributive intent? Will the undoubted opportunities for IT to be used to improve the lives and offset the disadvantages of physically disabled people be recognised and built upon by social welfare agencies?

— How far will new communities of interest emerge spontaneously from the public, and how far will they be the product of organisations with the financial power and professional skill to define and package issues in particular ways? Will a more technically literate population be able to marshall counter-expertise to tackle issues posed by information society (e.g. data privacy and surveillance)?

— How far will the expansion of computing and telecommunications power within the home lead to new forms of privatisation of family life, of individualisation of family members one from another, of personal 'addiction' to fantasy worlds presented with increasing verisimilitude, and of the strengthening of boundaries between subcultures, rather than to interpersonal contact that involves mutual reliance, problem-solving, and understanding?

— How will concerns about civil liberties and privacy be handled in a world in which the volumes of data concerning individuals, generated in the course of everyday life (let alone intentional surveillance), are such as to make data protection legislation cumbersome and traditional professional regulations about confidentiality obsolete?

— How in practice will the contrasting pressures of centralisation and decentralisation—both of which IT can implement—be reconciled? How will regional disparities be reflected in political action?

While the problems that have been discussed are not inevitable, there is no point in claiming that specific policy choices will lead to one or other form of information society. The patterns of development that emerge—the features of the new or technological paradigm—involve *bounded* social choice. There are a number of important features of this:

(1) IT makes many new options available, but it is a material technology, not a magical apparatus capable of fulfilling every wish (or nightmare) on demand. Nevertheless, IT is an extremely malleable technology, which can be applied to many purposes and embodied in many forms.

(2) On the other hand, it is associated with a greater transnationalisation of economic activities, which may erode some 'protective' underpinnings of distinctive national economies and cultures, and of national political strategies.

(3) The choice of any one actor or set of actors (a nation, say) is strongly

conditioned by the choices of others, as are the results of choices: thus the pattern of development of this very malleable technology may be largely determined by international economic competition.

(4) All actors are making decisions under conditions of considerable uncertainty: even those with the best understanding of the technical aspects of a specific decision are often ignorant of many surrounding technological, social and organisational developments; and they will probably be even more unable to specify the innovations (and possibly subversions) in the use of installed equipment and services—which are a particularly marked feature of the learning processes around revolutionary innovations.

Thus, while choice does exist, its boundaries and consequences are uncertain to greater or lesser degrees, and the future is the result of the interaction of many choices (and revisions of choices). This suggests that policies and strategies will need to be flexible, and that technical prototyping and social experiments should play a more substantial role in guiding them. And since knowledge of social needs and market structures, and of innovations in everyday life as well as in R&D laboratories, is not the property of any elite, it is crucial that wide social participation be achieved in planning and evaluating such experiments.

It is difficult to summarise this book, but we can offer the following concluding thoughts. In one form or another Home Informatics are going to be a reality that we will all need to confront—as consumers and citizens, as clients and concerned individuals, as policymakers or as the subjects of policy. It is time for us to begin to do so as effectively as possible.

Notes

1. In Gershuny and Miles (1983) we used the term 'sociotechnical system' in much the same sense as 'technological paradigm' is being used here; see also Miles (1985).
2. Teleshopping might be an exception: while it would reduce demand for check-out and in-store staff, it would require delivery staff.
3. For a concise account of the 'regulation' approach as developed by French writers, see Petit (1986), who writes in the context of future developments in service sectors of the economy (and whose final chapters raise some of the issues of dualism discussed here); see also Blackburn et al. (1986) who relate the approach more closely to IT (and who also discuss IT challenges to public services). For an alternative approach to long-term trends in, and periods of, capitalist society, one that suggests additional lines to pursue and introduces the question of relations between the culture sphere and political economy in 'postmodernism', see Lash and Urry (1987). For a sympathetically critical approach to advocates of left-wing and green approaches to post-industrial (information?) society, see Frankel (1987): these advocates would sidestep many of the problems discussed in this chapter by more autarkic strategies.
4. It is perhaps too easy to generalise from the increased inequality that has been manifest in countries like Britain and the United States in the past decade; we

should note that not all Western countries have responded to the global economic crisis in the same way (for instance, Scandinavian countries have adopted training schemes as an alternative to unemployment and a means of upgrading the labour force to cope with new technological systems. But the potential for IT to displace many middle-level positions in the formal economy seems to be one that many employers are likely to seize, and studies of (current generations of) IT innovation tend to suggest that, while more positions tend to be upgraded than downgraded in this process, there is none the less a drift towards a labour force more differentiated between high-skill and low-skill jobs. (Though this need not necessarily be translated into a new class structure, since in principle individuals need not remain fixed in particular job locations and career trajectories.)

5. There are numerous other aspects of dualism that we cannot do more than touch on here: fortunately, most are less relevant to HI per se, concerning broader dimensions such as regional disparities (where the proposed countermeasures may involve, for example, the use of DBS to supplement localised cable systems, the establishment of regional teleports and resource centres, etc.).

6. Similar arguments are made concerning the potential for IT to refresh democratic structures and provide new channels for participatory politics: for a useful and critical review of arguments and evidence, see Arterton (1987).

7. The typology of modes of action presented in these paragraphs is based on Miles and Irvine (1982).

Bibliography

F.C. Arterton, 1987, *Teledemocracy: Can Technology Protect Democracy?* Newbury Park, Calif., Sage Publications.

E. Bates, 1986, Presentation to Home Informatics Workshop, London, 1986.

W.E. Bijker, T.P. Huges and T.J. Pinch (eds), 1987, *The Social Construction of Technological Systems*, Cambridge, Mass., MIT Press.

P. Blackburn, R. Coombes and K. Green, 1986, *Technology, Economic Growth and the Labour Process*, London, Macmillan.

F. Blackler and D. Oborne (eds), 1987, *Information Technology and People*, Letchworth, Herts., British Psychological Society, Cambridge, Mass., MIT Press.

D. Bosworth, 1987, 'Prices, Costs, and the Elasticity of Demand', in OECD, *Information Technology and Economic Prospects*, Paris, Organisation for Economic Cooperation and Development, Information Computer Communications Policy No. 12.

T. Bowling, 1986, 'Smart House', paper presented at the Home Informatics Workshop, London, 1986.

British Telecom, 1985, *Action for Disabled Customers*, London, British Telecom.

J. Brunner, 1969, *Stand on Zanzibar*, London, Macdonald Books.

M.A. Buckles, 1987, 'Interactive Fiction as Literature', *Byte*, May 1987, pp. 135–42.

Business Week, 1983, 'Telecommunications Liberalisation', reprinted in Forester (1985).

V. Cappechi, A. Pesce and M. Schiray, 1986 'Nouvelles Technologies et Vie Quotidienne' (2 vols.) mimeo, University of Bologna and CIRED, Paris, recherche réalisée par la Convention no. 85218 avec la Commission des Communautés Européenes, Directions Générale des Affaires Sociales de le Main d'Oeuvre et de l'Education, Brussels.

A. Cawson, P. Holmes and A. Stevens, 1986, 'The interaction between Firms and the State in France: The Telecommunications and Consumer Electronics Sectors', Falmer, Brighton, University of Sussex, Working Paper Series on Government–Industry Relations, No. 4.

CD-I News, 1986, 'CD-ROM, CD-I Controversy Erupts in New York, London', December 1986 **1**, No. 2, p. 4.

CNET, 1983, *Images Pour Le Cable*, Paris, La Documentation Française.

R. Coombs, P. Saviotti and V. Walsh, 1987, *Economics and Technological Change*, London, Macmillan.

T.A. Defanti, 1984, 'The Mass Impact of Videogame Technology', *Advances in Computers*, New York, Academic Press, **23**.

B. Easlea, 1984, *Fathering the Unthinkable*, London, Pluto Press.

J. Evans, J. Hartley, J. Simnett, M. Gibbons and S. Metcalfe, 1983, *The Development of Cable Networks in the UK*, London, Technical Change Centre.

E.A. Feigenbaum and P. McCorduck, 1983, *The Fifth Generation*, Reading, Mass., Addison-Wesley.

R. Finnegan, G. Salaman and K. Thompson (eds), 1987, *Information Technology: Social Issues*, Sevenoaks, Kent, Hodder & Stoughton.

T. Forester (ed.), 1985, *The Information Technology Revolution*, Oxford, Basil Blackwell.

T. Forester, 1987, *High-Tech Society*, London, MIT Press.

B. Fox, 1987a, 'Compact Disc Video hits the streets . . . but in more ways than one', *New Scientist*, 13 March 1987, p. 28.

B. Fox, 1987b, 'War declared on Tape Pirates . . . How the Proof of the Pudding went Wrong', *New Scientist*, 14 May 1987, p. 38.

B. Frankel, 1987, *The Post-Industrial Utopians*, Cambridge, Polity Press.

C. Freeman, 1982, *The Economics of Industrial Innovation*, London, Frances Pinter.

C. Freeman, J. Clark and L.L.G. Soete, 1982, *Technical Change and Unemployment*, London, Frances Pinter.

C. Freeman and C. Perez, 1986, 'The Diffusion of Technological Innovations and Changes of Techno-economic Paradigm', paper presented at IFIAS Venice conference. (mimeo, Science Policy Research Unit)

J. Gershuny, 1977, *After Industrial Society: The Emerging Self-service Economy*, London, Macmillan.

J. Gershuny, 1986, 'Time-Use Patterns and the Future of Work', paper presented at Home Informatics Workshop, London, 1986.

J. Gershuny and I. Miles, 1983, *The New Service Economy*, London, Frances Pinter.

GLC, 1986, *The London Industrial Strategy*, London, Greater London Council.

D. Gleave, (ed.) 1986, *IRIS: a UK Inventory*, London, Technical Change Centre.

GLEB, 1986, *New Technology Networks*, London, Greater London Enterprise Board.

B. Guile, 1986, 'Investigation of a Transaction-Cost Approach to Market Failures in the Development and Diffusion of Manufacturing Technologies', paper presented at Annual Meeting of Association for Public Policy Analysis and Management, Austin, Texas, October–November 1986.

L. Haddon, 1987, 'The Future of the Micro: the continuing debate'; (mimeo) draft chapter for D.Phil. dissertation, Imperial College, London.

R.L. Hamblin, R.B. Jacobson and J.L.L. Miller, 1974, *A Mathematical Model of Social Change*, New York, Wiley-Interscience.

J. Hartley, J.S. Metcalfe, J. Evans, J. Simnett, L. Georghiou and M. Gibbons, 1985 *Public Acceptance of New Technologies: New Communications Technology and the Consumer*, Manchester, PREST, University of Manchester.

J. Hendry, 1972, 'The Three Parameter Approval to Long Range Forecasting', *Long Range Planning*, (March), pp. 40–5.

J. Hills, 1986, *Deregulating Telecoms*, London, Frances Pinter.

Information Dynamics Limited, 1986, *Impact of Interconnected National PTT Data Networks on the Users of European Information Services*, Luxembourg, European Commission.

ITAP, 1982, *The Cabling of Britain*, London, HMSO.

R.S. Iwaasa, 1985, 'Télématique grand public: l'information ou la communication', *Le Bulletin de l'IDATE*, Janvier 1985, no. 18, pp. 43–51.

R.S. Iwaasa, 1986, 'Convivial Messaging Systems: keys for domestic telematics', paper presented at Home Informatics Workshop, London, 1986.

F. Kappetyn, 1986, Presentation at the Homes Informatics Workshop, London, 1986.

T. Kaye, 1986, 'Teletel: a Case-Study of Interactive Videotex', draft prepared for

DT200 'An Introduction to Information Technology', Milton Keynes, Open University.

J.J. Keller, K. Dreyfac and R. Mitchell, 1986, 'The Rewiring of America', *Business Week*, 15 September 1986, pp. 102–7.

S. Lash and J. Urry, 1987, *The End of Organized Capitalism*, Cambridge, Polity Press.

D. MacKenzie and J. Wajcman (eds), 1985, *The Social Shaping of Technology*, Milton Keynes, Open University Press.

Mackintosh International, 1984, *The European Consumer Electronics Industry*, Luton, Mackintosh International, published by European Commission as IV/247/84-EN in Working Papers on Evolution of Concentration and Competition.

I. Mackintosh, 1986, *Sunrise Europe*, Oxford, Basil Blackwell.

R. Macleod (ed.), 1986, *Technology and the Human Prospect*, London, Frances Pinter.

H. Maurer, 1986, 'Distance Education via Interactive Telecommunications', paper presented at Home Informatics Workshop, London, November 1986.

R. Mayntz and V. Schneider, 1987, 'Interactive Telecommunications: the case of videotex in Germany, France and Great Britain', paper presented at Conference on 'Development of Large Technical Systems', Cologne, November 1987.

W.H. Melody, 1986, 'Telecommunication—policy directions for the technology and information services' in *Oxford Surveys in Information Technology vol. 3*, London, Oxford University Press.

S. Metcalfe, 1986, 'Technological innovation and the Competitive Process', in P. Hall (ed.) *Technology, Innovation and Economic Policy*, Oxford, Philip Allan.

I. Miles, 1985, 'The New Post-Industrial State', *Futures* **17** No. 6, pp. 588–617.

I. Miles and J. Gershuny, 1987, *Work in Information Society* (mimeo) SPRU, a report to the Joseph Rowntree Memorial Trust, being revised for book publication.

I. Miles and J. Irvine, 1982, *The Poverty of Progress*, Oxford, Pergamon Press.

I. Miles, H. Rush, K. Turner and J. Bessant, 1988 forthcoming, *Information Horizons*, Aldershot, Edward Elgar.

D. Moralee, 1985, 'Paving the Way to All-Digital Broadcasting', *Electronics and Power*, June 1985, pp. 435–44.

G. Murdock, P. Hartmann and P. Grey, 1985 'Everyday Innovations' in *Public Acceptance of New Technologies, vol. 2: Appendices I–V*, University of Manchester, PREST.

NEDO, 1986, *IT Futures*, London, National Economic Development Office, IT Economic Development Committee.

NEDO, 1987, *Automating the Home . . . Now and Tomorrow* (conference papers), London, National Economic Development Office.

C. Perez, 1983, 'Structural Change and the Assimilation of New Technologies in the Economic and Social Systems', *Futures*, October, pp. 357–75.

C. Perez, 1985, 'Microelectronics, Long Waves and World Development', *World Development* **13**, No. 3 (March).

P. Petit, 1986, *Slow Growth and the Service Economy*, London, Frances Pinter.

Philips, 1986, *CD ROM: Optical Technology Serving Electronic Publishing*, New York, Philips Subsystems and Peripherals Inc.

Philips, 1987, *MAC: Tomorrow's Television World*, Eindhoven, Philips Consumer Electronics, Satellite TV Department.

Phosphor Products, 1986, *Phosphor Products (Information pack)* Upton, Poole, Dorset, Phosphor Products Co. Ltd.

R.E. Poill, 1968, *A Test of the Classical Product Life Cycle by Means of Actual Sales*

Histories, unpublished doctoral dissertation, University of Pennsylvania (as cited by Robertson, 1971).

C. Presvelou, 1986a, *Households, the Home Computer and Related Services in the Netherlands*, Brussels, European Commission, FAST Programme paper No. 94.

C. Presvelou, 1986b, 'The use of New Information Technologies in Dutch Households', paper presented at Home Informatics Workshop, London, November 1986.

Psion Ltd., 1986, *Psion Organiser II: the machine that thinks with you* (promotional leaflet), London, Psion Ltd.

C. Rapoport, 1986, 'How Nintendo aims to Play the World', *The Financial Times*, 13 November 1986.

L. Raun and D. Thomas, 1987, 'Philips, Sony consider mini-compact disc', *The Financial Times*, 6 February 1987, p. 4.

T.S. Robertson, 1971, *Innovative Behavior and Communication*, New York, Holt, Rinehart & Winston.

E.M. Rogers, 1962, *Diffusion of Innovations*, New York, Free Press.

E.M. Rogers, 1986, *Communications Technology*, New York, Free Press.

E. Rothschild, 1974, *Paradise Lost: The Decline of the Auto-industrial Age*, London, Allen Lane.

N. Russel, 1986, 'Prestel—the Rational Solution?', paper presented at Home Informatics Workshop, London, 1986.

M. Schatz-Bergfeld, 1986, 'The Northrhine-Westphalia Programme "Man and Technology"—an innovative political conception to shape technology in a socially compatible way . . .', paper presented at Home Informatics Workshop, London, 1986.

J. Schofield, 1984, 'How to Bend your Mind to Suggestive Proposals', *The Guardian* (London), 11 October 1984, p. 17.

J. Schofield, 1987a, 'Robots Up and Running', *The Guardian* (London), 10 September 1987, p. 15.

J. Schofield, 1987b, 'The Circuits of Glory lead frequently to the Grave', *The Guardian* (London), 8 January 1987, Computer Section.

C. Sinha, 1987, 'Machines to get on with', *The Guardian* (London), 20 July 1987, p. 15.

M.S. Snow and M. Jussawalla, 1986, 'Background and Issues: Impact of Information Technology on Domestic Industrial Structure—Deregulation Trends in OECD Countries', paper presented at TIDE 2000 Second Symposium, East–West Center, Honolulu, May 1986.

P. Spinks, 1985, 'The Micro that tells you where to go', *The Guardian* (London), 26 September 1985.

W. Stallings, 1984, 'The Integrated Services Digital Network', *Datamation*, (December), Figure 4.

G. Thomas and I. Miles, 1986, *Technological Change and the Provision of Services to Households*, Brussels, European Commission, FAST Programme report.

G. Thomas and I. Miles, 1987, 'The Emergence of Interactive Services: a progress report' (mimeo), SPRU, University of Sussex, report to the Leverhulme Trust.

J. Tunstall, 1986, *Communications Deregulation*, Oxford, Basil Blackwell.

S. Turkle, 1985, *The Second Self*, London, Grafton Books.

S. R. Turner, 1986a, 'The Coding of Pictures, Sound and Graphics in CD-ROM for Consumer Applications', paper presented at 1986 IEEE International Conference on Consumer Electronics.

S. R. Turner, 1986b, Presentation to Home Informatics Workshop, London 1986.

J. Tydeman and E. J. Keim, 1986, *New Media in Europe*, London, McGraw-Hill.

N. Valery, 1977, 'Spare a Byte for the Family', *New Scientist*, 19 May 1977, pp. 405–6.

N. P. Vitalari and A. Venkatesh, 1987, 'In-home Computing and Information Services', *Telecommunications Policy*, March 1987, pp. 65–81.

A. Watson Brown, 1987, 'The Campaign for High Definition Television', *Euro-Asia Business Review*, **6**, No. 2, pp. 3–11.

S. Watts, 1986, 'So How Are You Feeling Today, Building?', *Computer Weekly*, 27 February 1986, p. 30.

C. Weston, 1986, Presentation to Home Informatics Workshop, London, 1986.

R. Whymant, 1987, 'In Lieu of Doctor—Tokyo Style', *The Daily Telegraph* (London), 27 May 1987, p. 1.

D. Wield, 1987, *The Politics of Technological Innovation*, Milton Keynes, Open University, Technology Policy Group Occasional Paper No. 10.

R. Williams and S. Mills, 1986, *Public Acceptance of New Technologies: An International Review*, London, Croom Helm.

Index